WALKING IN DEVON

Walkers on the cliff path below Sharp Tor, Near Bolt Head. (Walk 17)

WALKING IN DEVON

by

David Woodthorpe

CICERONE PRESS
MILNTHORPE, CUMBRIA

© David Woodthorpe 1996
ISBN 1 85284 223 7
A catalogue record for this book is available from the British Library

To Mum and Dad

ACKNOWLEDGEMENTS

Grateful thanks go to the editor of the *Express* and *Echo*, Rachel Campey, for her advice, encouragement and for agreeing in autumn 1991 to print the first of a series of walks which form the core of this book. Thanks also to Dave Murdock and Jane Leigh who had the dubious privilege of subbing my copy. Final thanks go to the Rights of Way section of Devon County Council who kindly allowed me access to their maps.

Front Cover: On the cliffs near Windbury Point.
Photo: W. Unsworth

CONTENTS

DEVON WALK FINDER

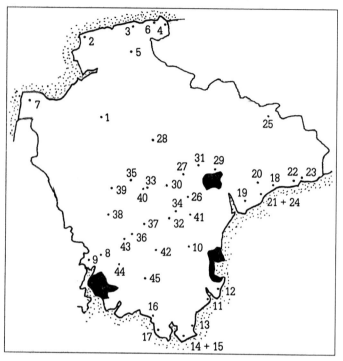

INTRODUCTION

Devon's variety of scenery is unmatched anywhere else in Britain. At its centre are the bleak high moors and tors of Dartmoor - Devon's granite heartland. In the east where it greets Dorset, heath wanders into chalk downland and flint-napped cottages echoing Hampshire and Sussex. Moving west are the great red sandstone cliffs which stretch round the coast to the edge of Torbay. Further south the drowned river valleys or rias of Dartmouth, Salcombe-Kingsbridge and Plymouth Sound itself. To the 120 miles of southern coastline washed by the English Channel, can be added the 60 miles of northern coast, much of it hammered by the Atlantic. In the far north-west, as on Dartmoor, place names, church patron saints and field shapes speak more of the Celts than of the Saxon invaders which supplanted them in so much of the county. Where the north coast turns to face South Wales, it meets Exmoor's 1000 feet high cliffs dropping to the sea in great ladders of scree and vicious V-shaped river valleys.

In between lies countryside whose reputation for unspoilt beauty stretches far beyond England. Half of the country's mud built or cob cottages are to be found in Devon, where the thatched roof is a feature, at least in part, of almost every village. Small steep sided valleys or combes drained by thin brooks are studded with isolated farmsteads, especially in Mid Devon. Large parts of the county, particularly the north and west, have seen only limited urban development, the majority of which has been concentrated in the south on Plymouth, Exeter and Torbay. Devon still remains predominantly a rural county and the best way to see it is on foot.

AROUND DEVON ON FOOT - USING THIS GUIDE
This book includes 45 walks ranging from 1.5 to 14 miles in length. All but one of the walks are round routes. They have been designed with the idea of avoiding roads wherever possible - my feeling is that if you are going to go by road you might as well cycle or drive. Where roads form part of any route they are usually country lanes and then only employed because there is no suitable footpath, bridleway or unadopted track alternative.

For the coast walker the book includes 16 routes, 15 of which are round walks. In this way the chore of simply retracing your steps at the end of a coastal tramp is avoided. Instead the inland loops hold much, if not as much excitement as the coast itself.

When faced with Dartmoor's often featureless moorland many walkers turn aside, fearful lest the weather turns and they find themselves lost in mist with no clear way home. Of the 14 Dartmoor routes explained here, 10 are over what is known as the high moor. Each of these follows distinct landscape features, usually rivers, and 5 are specially designed "Ridge and River" routes.

As the name suggests these walks follow a ridge and river out and back or vice versa. Walkers new to Dartmoor as well as the more experienced are able to follow these bold features well into the high moor. In this way it is possible to build up confidence before ranging across great swathes of open moorland.

Each walk is divided into a "Directions" box and text. Directions include details of the walk's start, an outline of the type of walking and length, with a rough idea of time it will take for an averagely fit person who takes short breaks on the way. Other information includes basic advice of how to get to the start, where to park, refreshments if any on the route, and in some instances suggested bus links, as well as a recommended Ordnance Survey map.

Where any Dartmoor walk passes through an official army firing range on the north moor these are noted. The walker should check in advance whether there is any firing by ringing the pre-recorded range information line on Exeter 70164/Okehampton 52939/Plymouth 501478/Torquay 294592. Up to the minute firing information can be had daily from Okehampton Army Camp on (01837) 52241/42 extension 3210.

Remember metal objects should never be picked up from an army range - they could be unexploded shells.

The route text comes in two parts. The italic type is information relating to features met on the walk, while the normal type gives details about the actual path route, such as where you might cross a stile or turn left through a gate.

Each walk is accompanied by a sketch map. This acts as a basic guide but is designed to be used in conjunction with the OS map recommended under "Directions".

THE WELL DRESSED WALKER

Any regular walker will know what they are most comfortable wearing but for the new walker here are a few clothing tips.

It is better to wear a number of thin layers of clothing rather than one or two thick ones. Lots of layers trap warmth and they allow finer temperature regulation. This is particularly pertinent on Dartmoor where the walker who stops after a hard stretch and peels off a thick layer of clothing runs the risk of rapidly chilling in a cold wind.

It goes without saying that waterproofs, both top and bottom, are essential in Devon. Breathable fabrics which "wick" sweat away from the skin are to be recommended but they do not come cheap and their effectiveness is dependent on the other clothes you wear. Cotton has a tendency to hold moisture next to the body. This is not a problem on a hot sunny day when it is quickly evaporated. It does become a problem if it is cold, when the moisture rapidly chills against the skin, especially if you stop moving. For this reason, and for the amount of water they retain if they ever get wet, jeans should always be avoided.

Wear stout shoes or walking boots. On Dartmoor walking boots which grip the ankle firmly are a must as they cut down the risk of sprains and twists when crossing tussocky or clitter covered ground. Remember to take whatever refreshments you will need on the walk if there are none on the route.

WALKING ON DARTMOOR AND EXMOOR

The case for specialist walking kit is reinforced by the changeable conditions experienced on Dartmoor and Exmoor. A hot sunny day can become one of cold wind and driving rain or worse in minutes.

Go prepared. Always take emergency rations and water, waterproofs and, it goes without saying in winter, woolly hat, gloves and scarf. Take a compass and know how to use it. Leave details of where you are walking with family and friends and a likely return time so that in the event of your non-reappearance they can alert the mountain rescue and emergency services.

As explained above many of the moorland routes follow bold landscape features like ridges and rivers. If you do ever become lost remember that if you walk downhill you will eventually meet a stream or river, which, if followed downstream will carry you off the moor.

CLIMATE, GEOLOGY, FLORA AND FAUNA

Devon is by any standards wet. In an average year Dartmoor catches 90 inches of rain and 100 inches at Princetown (1400 feet) is not unknown, while Exmoor collects 70 inches. In the east, after Dartmoor has already taken much from the prevailing westerlies, rainfall drops to 32 inches at Exeter. Both coasts typically receive 40-45 inches.

The county is something of a geologist's paradise. Large areas of rock, particularly round the coast and on Dartmoor, are exposed. The county's highest point is High Willhays at 2030 feet and Dartmoor's poorly drained granite ensures peaty acid soils. In the far east of the county a small area of chalk between Seaton and Branscombe gives way to greensand, clays and Permian marls. The Budleigh Salterton Pebble Beds support distinctive heathland hill tops while the marls mark rich grassland.

Stretching east, south to Paignton and in a western tongue north of Okehampton are the Permian New Red Sandstone series of rocks which were laid down millions of years ago under desert conditions. These rocks form the high cliffs and red soils of east and south Devon, which have given Devon the reputation of being a "Red" county - a reputation probably based upon the images of early 20th century rail posters promoting Torbay, or the English Riviera as it likes to be known.

Slates and sandstones dominate the rather windswept South Hams. At Start and Prawle Points occur Devon's oldest rocks, green, mica and hornblende schists.

As a result of the emergence of the South West granite batholith many rocks round the fringe of Dartmoor underwent metamorphosis. The granite contains metal bearing lodes, especially tin, but round its margin other metals are found. Lead, silver, manganese and iron were all mined from the flanks of the Teign Valley. The western moorland edge along the Tamar supported even greater deposits. Round Tavistock huge finds of copper were discovered and mined during the latter half of the 19th century.

Degraded and decomposed weathered granite formed fine

china and ball clays, collecting in basins at Lee Moor on the south-western edge of Dartmoor (china clay) and on the eastern edge in the Bovey Basin (ball clay), along with sands and gravels.

The main body of the county running from Hartland in the west to the edge of Exeter in the east is made up of the Culm Measures, shales which have weathered to produce characteristic and often poor agricultural soils.

In the north slates, as at jagged Morte Point, and volcanic rocks dominate, continuing at different ages of deposition to mark the landscape of both the coast and Exmoor.

Devon remains primarily a pastoral dairy county, fields divided by high hedges and mixed woodland, supporting a wide range of plant and animal species. All the usual mammals of field and wood occur - voles, shrew, mice, rabbits, squirrels, badgers and foxes. Red deer occur on Exmoor and fallow deer elsewhere. After years of persecution the otter is making a come-back, especially along the little-disturbed northern rivers, though escaped mink which are thriving in the wild are hunted in the otter's place.

For reptiles the adder or viper with its distinctive black diamond back can be found across the county including Dartmoor. Quickly heated sandy heathland is a favourite "haunt" where the grass snake and slow worm, actually a legless lizard, and common lizard also occur.

Birds out of the ordinary which Devon supports include the red grouse, golden plover and curlew on Dartmoor, where the wheatear and skylark are common. The dipper is to be found on most fast flowing freshwater moorland streams, as is the grey wagtail. The red kite has been known to stop at Soussons Down on Dartmoor during its migration flight from North Africa to the Welsh Marches.

The nightjar patrols East Devon's heaths, where, as on other heathland and around the rougher stretches of coast, the stonechat and yellowhammer may also be found. The heron is common wherever there is water, very occasionally accompanied by a rare visitor, the little egret. Coots, moorhens and swans are resident while a few freshwater lakes, including Slapton Ley in the south of the county, support the great crested grebe.

Cormorants, shags, guillemots, fulmar and oyster catchers, as well as ubiquitous gulls of various types, can be found at sites round the coast. The Exe estuary is especially noted for its winter population of avocets.

Woodland birds include the green and great spotted woodpeckers, the nuthatch and gold crest. Swallows and house martins nest in summer. The largest member of the hawk family, the buzzard, soars over field and moor. The kestrel and sparrow hawk are represented along with the rare and spectacular peregrine falcon.

WHEREVER YOU GO FOLLOW THE COUNTRY CODE

Enjoy the countryside and respect its life and work.
Guard against all risk of fire.
Fasten all gates.
Keep your dogs under close control.
Keep to public paths across farmland.
Use gates and stiles to cross fences, hedges and walls.
Leave livestock, crops and machinery alone.
Take your litter home.
Help to keep all water clean.
Protect wildlife, plants and trees.
Take special care on country roads.
Make no unnecessary noise.

Or in the eloquent words of naturalist David Bellamy, take nothing but photos, leave nothing but footprints.

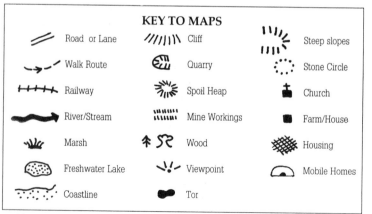

KEY TO MAPS

Road or Lane	Cliff	Steep slopes
Walk Route	Quarry	Stone Circle
Railway	Spoil Heap	Church
River/Stream	Mine Workings	Farm/House
Marsh	Wood	Housing
Freshwater Lake	Viewpoint	Mobile Homes
Coastline	Tor	

The Walks

---

1. NORTH DEVON
The quiet country - Beaford along the banks of the River Torridge - 1.5 miles

---

Directions

Start: Beaford village centre off the B3220 a few miles south-east of Great Torrington.

Outline and
walk length: A short gentle stroll of 1.5 miles along the banks of the River Torridge. One short climb. Allow an hour and a half depending on nature watching.

Getting there: From the B3220 or following the signs from the A386.

Parking: In the main part of the village on the road leading to Beaford Bridge; south-west of the B3220.

Refreshments: Pub in Beaford.

Map: OS 1:50,000 Barnstaple and Ilfracombe; Landranger no. 180.

Early evening waning into dusk is often the best time to see wildlife. Even in high summer when scarcely any animal except the cawing crow stirs during the day, come dusk all sorts of sights and sounds shuffle into activity.

This walk offers a short after-work stroll to the banks of the Torridge where the quiet, pausing walker may catch the wood heaving into its night-time life.

Sleepy Beaford perches above the River Torridge on the fringe of North Devon. It boasts a church, a pub and rather surprisingly a small arts centre.

To begin the walk head away from the B3220 as if you are walking towards Beaford Bridge on the Torridge. You will pass a small estate of fairly modern bungalows on the left, after which go right down a lane towards Abbot's Hill Hotel. You will shortly pass Beaford Arts Centre on the right. As the lane falls so the wooded

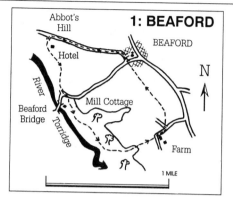

1: BEAFORD

Abbot's Hill

BEAFORD

Hotel

River Torridge

Mill Cottage

Beaford Bridge

Farm

N

1 MILE

slopes of the Torridge rear into sight.

Immediately past the Abbot's Hill Hotel turn left down a track. The hotel will now be on your left with another house on your right. The track falls swiftly into woods before coming out onto a lane. To your right is Mill Cottage and below it Beaford Bridge.

Instead, go left up the lane a short way before turning right onto a signposted footpath and entering the dense deciduous woods. The path follows the Torridge upstream.

In the summer of 1995 the Torridge scarcely deserved the title of a river, so low was its flow. Yet the deathly hush of a hot August day gave way to an almost audible sigh from the beech and oak as the unrelenting sun finally waned in the evening.

First one, then two brilliant flashes of iridescent electric blue darted along the river - kingfishers - jabbing tiny wriggling silver fish from where the river squeezed round a fallen beech. As I leant closer for a better view a surprised heron hidden by the bank's overhang heaved itself languidly into the sultry air. As I moved on a dark thick-coated mink slipped across the path.

Shortly before the wood gives way to a field the path bears left uphill. Ignore the temptation to follow the narrow paths off to the left of the path you are now on - these lead back into the wood. Cross a stile into a field which drops away sharply to your right. Keep the hedge on your left as you walk uphill. At the next gate on your left go through it and continue uphill along a track. Follow the track through another gate, across another field and gate onto a lane.

Leaving behind a farm and house on the right follow the lane uphill, turning left just past a row of conifers - the lane marked with a sign stating "A.M Jennings, North Harepath, No Travellers". A few yards along the lane go right down a signposted footpath, over a stile and crossing a grassy field to a gate and stile. Over the stile cross a track and another stile into still another field following the hedge on your right.

A couple more stiles while following this hedge and then across a small field will lead you back through the small estate of bungalows passed earlier on the edge of Beaford.

---

2. NORTH DEVON:
Reaching out to Lundy along the Mortehoe coastline - 7 miles

Directions

Start:	Mortehoe, west of Ilfracombe, in the far north-west corner of Devon.
Outline and walk length:	A coastal walk into the teeth of the Atlantic. Relatively easy going for a 7 mile cliff route, taking a comfortable four to five hours depending on breaks.
Parking:	Car park on left as you enter Mortehoe from the east.
Refreshments:	In Mortehoe three pubs, three restaurants, fish and chip shop, food store and post office. In Lee one pub and a cottage selling teas, ice cream etc.
Map:	OS 1:50,000 Barnstaple and Ilfracombe; Landranger no. 180, though a 1:25,000 would help for negotiating the fields.

The deadly Morte Stone lying off Morte Point claimed five ships in the winter of 1852 alone. The jagged, shiny surfaces of the Morte Slate have proved treacherous to vessels down the centuries. Yet despite this coastline's predilection for shipwrecking Mortehoe's name is not derived from the French mort *meaning death.*

Mortehoe is a peaceful slate village, consisting of a few substantial buildings and two huddled rows of whitewashed cottages. Its most notable feature is the slate built church of St. Mary, with its squat tower dating from 1270. Inside is a glittering Victorian mosaic and the pew ends are intricately carved. The village's restaurants and pubs thrive on the summer trade but Mortehoe remains unspoilt.

Turn left out of the car park opposite the petrol station at the entrance to Mortehoe. Then immediately right down the road next to the post office, signposted to North Morte Farm. Walk to the road's end, and at the gate take the middle footpath through the campsite.

The footpath passes through Easewell Farm, and you should pass the washing block on your right before bearing slightly left between a green painted building and wall, signposted to Lee. On the other side you will once again be back upon grass, on your right a duck pond.

Go through the gate opposite, turning left immediately before Yarde Farm. Uphill between hedges, go through another gate then, keeping the hedge on the left, over a stile, through another field and gate, turning left onto the lane that runs downhill to Damage Barton.

Look out for the sweeping white blades of a large wind generator on one of the hills nearby.

Pass Damage Barton, a farm with a friendly collie. Go right immediately after the last ruined slate farm building. The path bears

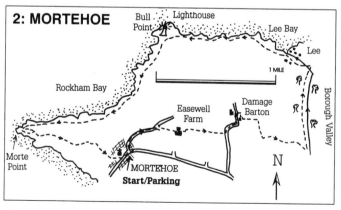

Layers of nearly perpendicular rock strata form the cliffs framing Lee Cove

left then right diagonally uphill, waymarked with yellow arrows and running back behind Damage Barton. At the wall, with Damage Barton on your right, go left uphill, through a gate and into a field of grass and gorse. The path levels out and you should head broadly straight on.

When you reach an opening in the hedge and wall on your left, turn right uphill, then left to the gate marked with a yellow arrow. Through the gate bear right diagonally across the field. Cross a stile then head slightly right through another field to the stile opposite. Cross the lane into a final field, walking across again and aiming for the dip, another stile over a fence, and then the steep and in places slippery path falling into Borough Valley.

Borough Valley is thickly wooded with coniferous trees on the eastern and deciduous on the western sides. Swaying ash splash sunlight across the woodland floor whose air is dank yet richly laden with perfumed flowers. Delicately fronded ferns curl from the damp gloomy places, and buddleia heavily scent the air as the path passes in turn through thicket, rhododendron, beech and oak.

At the path's foot turn left, taking the lower of the two footpaths signposted to Lee. You should follow the path out of the woods where it crosses the valley's stream and, once over a stile, keep the wall on your right to a gate. From there exit a small grassy field, and turn left onto a lane, past a hedge of red fuchsia and Chapel Cottage, which will bring you to Lee Bay.

Lee is a scattered settlement. A few old silver slated fishing cottages surround the bay supplemented by the second homes of well-to-do turn of the century gentry and merchants. When the tide recedes the bay reveals a little sand and much rock with sealife lurking in its pools. The scent of rotting bladderwrack should only add to your stock of memories.

To follow the coast path to Morte Point head west. Walk up the lane leading from the beach, turning right on to National Trust owned land. You are soon high above Lee and from Sandy Cove you can see the chunks of rock the Atlantic has bitten from the opposing cliff.

Various paths can be taken through what was a golf course: they meet up as you go west then fall to a small cove where oyster catchers shrill their call. Climbing the steep path ahead look back to see the upstanding jagged lines of slate like a shark's interminable rows of teeth. The path follows the cliff down another steep section then climbs again before arriving at Bull Point Lighthouse.

Looking north on a clear day the Gower Peninsula stretches out its knobbly thumb into the white-flecked blue of the Bristol Channel.

The path runs southward, skirting a rock fall of slate at Rockham Bay, before once again turning into the west and running out to Morte Point.

Here you are suddenly exposed to the full roar of the Atlantic, an unbridled place. Offshore, flat-topped and brooding like some enormous aircraft carrier is the island of Lundy. Look south across the sweep of Morte Bay to the half submerged "molar" of Baggy Point and beyond that Hartland Point. With the sea heaving and surging it is a mesmerising spot.

Mortehoe is now only a short walk away. It is possible to return inland via the spine of the Point. Or walk along the cliff a short way, rejoining the central path running back to an isolated walled cemetery and thence by the lane into the centre of the village.

---

3. NORTH DEVON:
Along the high cliffs between Heddon's Mouth and Woody Bay - 7 miles

Directions

Start: Hunter's Inn in the valley of the River Heddon between Lynton and Combe Martin.

Outline and
walk length: An easy to follow, clearly marked route over the cliffs and scree slopes of the North Devon coast between Heddon's Mouth and Woody Bay. Allow four to five hours for the 7 mile walk - up to an hour less if you skip the drop and steep climb from Woody Bay itself. The lower path from Heddon's Mouth to Woody Bay is rather exposed though not right on the cliff edge. The walk involves a couple of stiff climbs and an especially long one from Woody Bay.

Parking: National Trust car park with toilets, on left, just before Hunter's Inn.

Refreshments: In the Heddon Valley Hunter's Inn which is open all day and serves coffee and cream teas. There's also an ice cream shop. Otherwise none on walk.

Map: OS 1:25,000 Exmoor; Outdoor Leisure no. 9 or OS 1:50,000 Barnstaple and Ilfracombe which provides enough detail as the paths are clearly marked.

The heather-clad downs of the North Devon coast reach over 1000 feet in height within half a mile of the sea. Flat topped, like giant molars, precipitous scree strewn valleys separate each immense "tooth" in the landscape's jaw. This is a coastline of dramatic winding paths weaving across cliff faces to small gritty coves. No great headlands or bays gouge this coast which presents a severe wall to Wales directly north across the Bristol Channel. The walking is as demanding as anywhere along Britain's coastline.

This walk down the valley of the River Heddon gives a perfect sample of this stretch of coast, with scree covered slopes, high but not over-exposed cliffs and, in Woody Bay, a classic north facing cove plunged into shadow by mid afternoon.

Leaving the car park, head towards Hunter's Inn. Go just to the right of the pub through a gate and then bear left where signposted to Heddon's Mouth a mile away. The path falls to the river which can be crossed by either of two bridges, should you wish to walk along one bank to its mouth and return by the other. Towards its mouth you will leave the shelter of the trees and Heddon's Mouth Cleave is revealed.

Sessile oaks grow thickly upon the slopes of the Heddon Valley. Emerging from their cover the sides fall from 800 feet in less than half a mile. Ladders of scree - loose rock, here called the Hangman Grits - bleed down the Cleave's sides forming cone shapes where they meet the valley base. At Heddon's Mouth the river can be crossed by a number of stepping stones. There is a small pebbly beach swallowed by the incoming tide, and a couple of limekilns. Here limestone and coal from South Wales were burnt to form lime for spreading on the acid soils of the area. In return timber was loaded for use as pit props in the Welsh mines.

Leaving Heddon's Mouth, turn round and retrace your steps, keeping the river on your right. After a short distance past the first footbridge you come to, bear left uphill, signposted to Woody Bay.

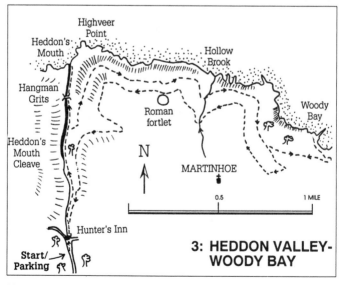

After a short but sharp climb you will reach Highveer Point.

A good rest halt with fine views back up the Heddon Valley and also west along the coast where the "molars" present a serrated edge to the sea. Catch your breath and look out for the buzzards, redstarts and pied flycatchers of this area. Out to sea you may spot some of the razorbills, kittiwakes, fulmars, and guillemots that nest on the cliffs below.

From Highveer Point follow the lower cliff path east. After skirting round another small headland the path turns a little inland over slopes composed largely of scree. It crosses Hollow Brook below its own cliff and waterfall.

Having left this impressive spot the path crosses, via a stile, into oak wood. The path widens and falls steadily and near its foot is a bench from where the view over Woody Bay can be enjoyed.

After another stile you have a choice. Go left and three-quarters of a mile downhill you will come to the foot of Woody Bay. Turn-of-the-century pleasure boat paddle steamers used to call at the now eroding pier. Nearby are a couple of limekilns and a slim beach. Be warned: it is a slog coming back up.

If the attraction is not great enough, go right, also uphill. Carry on, passing an individual house on the right, until another signposted official footpath branches off to the right. This you should follow uphill until you reach the upper cliff path which, turning right onto, will return you to Heddon Valley.

One bright baking summer's day I slumped to a halt on the upper cliff path, grateful to have beaten a bank of fog rolling along the Bristol Channel. The silent white shroud moved east, submerging Woody Bay and threading its chilly tentacles over cliff face and upstream valleys inland. Fog or not, the view is well worth pausing over.

The path now turns to the west, crossing a stile and passing round the Hollow Brook further upstream. This path can be followed back to the Heddon Valley.

A short diversion is possible up a path on the left which leads to an old Roman fortlet. Garrisoned by 65 to 85 soldiers between AD58 and 78, their task was sentry duty gazing across the Bristol Channel. Nowadays on a clear day South Wales is visible, billowing clouds of smoke marking the Port Talbot steelworks.

Returning to the main path, it soon re-enters the impressive Heddon Valley, falling steadily to rejoin the path just above Hunter's Inn.

---

4. NORTH DEVON:
Over Exmoor through "Doone Country" - Malmsmead and the River Badgworthy - 7 miles

---

Directions

Start: Malmsmead, east of Lynmouth, North Devon, in the Exmoor National Park.

Outline and
walk length: An easy-to-follow 7 mile walk up the banks of the River Badgworthy and across open moorland. A day out for *Lorna Doone* lovers, the route combines literary allusion, a river walk plus the big skies and featureless expanse of Exmoor. Allow four to five hours.

Getting there: From Lynmouth signposted right off the A39, through Brendon. From Porlock, signposted left off the A39 to Malmsmead.

Parking: National Park car park in Malmsmead. Toilets.

Refreshments: None on walk.

Map: OS Exmoor 1:25,000; Outdoor Leisure no. 9.

The Doones existed in local legend long before R.D. Blackmore collected the stories, upon which his famous book published in 1869 was based. Now literary hunters scour Exmoor for that 'authentic' 17th century valley setting. That the area between the River Badgworthy and Withycombe Ridge should be stamped Doone Country on the Ordnance Survey map might be a cause for their celebration. Anyone who thinks so should pause to consider the National Park information board in the official car park in Malmsmead, which reads: "Identification of the Doone Valley as the valley from Brendon through Malmsmead to Oare has been for the convenience of motor tours". So careful as you go with any notions of authenticity! That it is better to travel in the spirit of another's footsteps than in the imprint of their boots would here seem a good motto.

Originally called Molesmead - meaning "moles meadow" - Malmsmead is a cluster of farm buildings on the bank of the River Badgworthy hard against the county boundary with Somerset.

Leave the National Park car park, turn left through Malmsmead, ignoring the 30p shortcut scenic walk offered by a local farmer, and cross the 17th century packhorse bridge over the Badgworthy into Somerset.

After some 50 yards turn right down the metalled track and official footpath signposted to Cloud Farm. Just before Cloud Farm go right over the footbridge. Then left up the wide, well worn dusty signposted bridleway, walking upstream, the Badgworthy now on your left.

The valley sides are predominantly heather and bracken covered. After three-quarters of a mile you will come to an oak wood and pass a memorial stone to R.D. Blackmore.

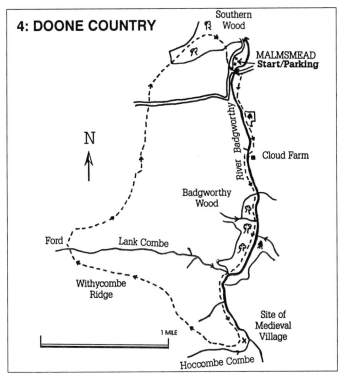

Doone Country - the Badgworthy just south of Lank Combe

Truly you are in the spirit of Lorna Doone country. Where literary strollers take bankside breaks, dabbling their hot summer toes in the cooling river.

The rock bed of the river has been folded at 45 degrees away from the water's flow and now the Badgworthy freely babbles over in a series of small waterfalls.

In places it glides across polished stone, elsewhere it is a still pool over a pebbly bed. The dark bottom gives the otherwise clear water a gloomy feel. Skittering through the shadows brown trout break the surface to gulp down carelessly alighted flies.

The oaks of Badgworthy Wood are captivating. Thin, scarcely mature boughs rise to 30 or 40 feet, with gentle twists and crooks, similar to those of Piles Copse on Dartmoor. Only a lush grass flourishes in the shade of their canopy. Grim conifers oppose them across the river.

Continue along through Badgworthy Wood until with the river still on your left, the path is carried over the stream issuing from Lank Combe, by a footbridge. Where the stream meets the

Badgworthy it has cut a fine river cliff, exposing the layers of rock.

A short excursion up Lank Combe will bring you to a series of three 30 degree steps in the bed over which the brook trips. These have been suggested as an inspiration for R.D. Blackmore's 'Glassy Steps' in Lorna Doone. *A very tranquil spot.*

Shortly after crossing Lank Combe the path plunges through a gloomy section overhung by rhododendrons with open pine woodland to the left of the Badgworthy. Follow the path upriver as it leaves the shade of wood and Himalayan transplants. The path is still wide, the valley sides climbing shapely moors clad in bracken. The walk's feeling becomes distinctly upland.

A mile distant is Hoccombe Combe, the reputed hidey-hole of the Doone clan. This area was associated with tales of robber families before Blackmore shepherded the locals' stories together.

The site of a medieval village where the Hoccombe meets the Badgworthy gives extra credence to the tale. The best time to explore the village is during winter or early spring before it is hidden by tall stands of bracken. The Hoccombe joins the river next to a beech-tree lined wall. A few hawthorns are dotted over the hillside.

Where the Badgworthy and Hoccombe meet turn right uphill, leaving the Badgworthy and passing a large mound on your left.

The path climbs steadily. After a few minutes you will come to a ruined farmstead on your right. The walls of the farmhouse are thrown down but not yet absorbed back into the moor, unlike those of the small fields around the enclosure. The path follows an old track from the farm, lined on both sides with a fine wall, entering the open moor through a gate.

As you climb Withycombe Ridge you will come to another gate. From the first, wide Exmoor views east can be had and south across a featureless hinterland. The broad, easily followed path continues its climb, the ground in places a little boggy. Finally it drops to Lankcombe Ford. A number of paths diverge but follow the route signposted to Malmsmead 2 miles distant; you will bear to the right somewhat. After a short rise you will reach another junction; bear right as signposted to Malmsmead.

Here the moor is covered in low heather - glorious in late summer and autumn. As you walk towards Malmsmead Hill so views north to the checkerboard hills immediately south of the Exmoor cliffs open out. On a clear day the Bristol Channel and South Wales are in view. The Port Talbot steel works belch smoke all year round and to the far west the Gower Peninsula jabs its thumb into the sea.

Gazing at Wales across the channel, I always feel, heightens the sense of separateness; of a distinctly different country over the water. A sense which in these islands is probably only possible elsewhere, if you stare from Dover to France or the Mull of Kintyre into Ireland. The hillside buzzes with insects. Overhead buzzards soar. Larks trill, tiny specks lost against the sky's brilliance.

Where the path branches follow the signs to Malmsmead. When you reach the road you have a straight choice. Either right to Malmsmead or straight over through the gate and onto the continuation of the bridleway you have always been following. The bridle route is to be recommended. It runs through attractive woodland and while it involves a drop and climb it is worth the effort. Through the gate take the left of the two tracks which soon begins to fall through Southern Wood.

The crowns of the topmost oaks are plucked clean of leaves - as if some giant, browsing herbivore has come grazing by. Across the steep valley side no vegetation has found a root hold and the rock has shattered - a nascent scree slope. The oak wood, like that of Badgworthy, is glorious in summer; with the sun streaming through it is a festival of dapple.

The path, wide and easy to follow, descends. In places there is plenty of loose rock so care should be taken not to lose your footing. Upon reaching the lane turn right and climb up a similar track through the wood. At the top there is coniferous stand on the left and Scots pine on the right. Over the top the path falls, passing through two gates back to the car park.

5. NORTH DEVON:
Bratton Fleming - Arlington Court - 9 miles

Directions

Start: On the road immediately west of St. Peter's church, Bratton Fleming, North Devon.

Outline and walk length: A delightful blend of North Devon hills and steep-sided sinuous valleys, with its heart the gardens and house of Arlington Court. Allow five hours without stopping at Arlington Court for the 9 miles, seven hours or more if you take a leisurely pace.

Getting there: From the A399 drop into Bratton Fleming, turning right immediately before the White Hart pub.

Parking: By the church.

Refreshments: Pub and shops in Bratton Fleming. Tea rooms at Arlington Court.

Map: OS 1:25,000 Exmoor; Outdoor Leisure no. 9 or OS 1:50,000 Barnstaple and Ilfracombe; Landranger no. 180.

Depending on your viewpoint Bratton Fleming either climbs the road to Exmoor or tumbles downhill towards the River Yeo. It boasts a couple of well kept chapels, one Baptist, one Methodist, in keeping with North Devon's tradition of religious nonconformism. The Church of St. Peter is rather more pleasant to look at from the outside than in. It has a low stone tower with clock dated 1897. Square shouldered slabs of slate, deeply inscribed, form the majority of graveyard memorials.

With the church on your left and village hall right, leave Bratton Fleming. At Button Hill Cross junction take the left fork, the lane signposted to Rye Park. After the South West Water depot leave the lane where it turns sharp right, instead carrying straight on downhill along a track. The track falls to Button Bridge over a stream which you should cross.

A leaping terrier battered itself against the side window of a van as I tramped past. Its owner emerged from the wood, all sawdust and snarling chain saw. We exchanged pleasantries and with the 'skia' call of a buzzard

29

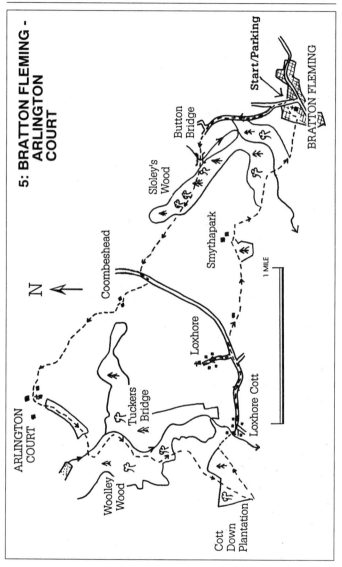

5: BRATTON FLEMING - ARLINGTON COURT

overhead, he returned to his felling.

The bank opposite is blanketed with conifers on the left, with an area clear-felled on the right. Remain on the track, which is officially an unadopted county road though unlikely to be passed by anything motorised with the exception of a four wheel drive - or tank. Shortly you will come to a junction of three paths. Take the middle one which climbs straight ahead. The "road" is alternatively muddy and in places smooth bare rock as it climbs through Sloley's Wood, emerging in a field via a gate. The OS 1:25,000 map shows no track to follow here but there is one on the ground which used to pass between high hedges, now sadly ripped out. Cross the field along the narrow path following the edge of the wire fence on your left. At its end you will reach a gate. Pass through and from here the final stretch between high hedges is marked on the OS map.

You will come to a lane. Turn left and shortly after passing Smythapark Farm on the left and Whitemoor Cottages on the right, you leave the lane via a footpath on the right signposted through a gate. The gate opens with some difficulty. Cross the field diagonally right towards two gates, passing through the left gate. Cross the next field, keeping to the left of the old farm buildings to a gate, again arrowed. Once through go right.

Named Coombeshead this was once a substantial farmstead. The farm and attendant cottages seem to have been built onto bare rock with their walls composed of loosely shuffled blocks of slate. Under the eaves are the muddy cups of swallow's nests, one lip pulled down to admit the adults. From inside come the fledglings' faint, plaintive cries.

The cottages are mostly empty, their windows eyeless sockets. Roof lines sag and there is an intense silence where past generations tilled the soil, loved, laughed and argued. If you want a vision of rural depopulation it is here.

As you pass through the farmstead keep left and follow the level track to a gate. Once through bear right across the long width of the field and keep the hedge on your right until you come to a footpath gate through which you pass into a short stretch of wood. The wooded flanks of the River Yeo are to the west.

After about 20 yards the path leaves the wood. Walk to the gate right of the house opposite. Ahead a row of fine beech trees and church tower at Arlington Court give the first hint of the architectural and horticultural surprises to come. At the gate an arrow points you right, passing a modern farm building on your left.

The track falls past what were Arlington Court's stables - note the heron with snake in beak topping the small dome. Just past the stables go left signposted "To the Church", passing a wonderful white painted wooden lattice gate.

Having passed the front of the church tower, lofty if not arrestingly interesting inside, turn right along the gravel path towards the house. If you are not stopping take the first fork 10 yards on the left by the information board.

The main part of Arlington Court was built in 1820 by Colonel John Chichester in "a severely plain Greek revival style", according to the National Trust estate guide. An enlarged hall and north wing were added in 1865 by the colonel's grandson, Sir Bruce Chichester, whose daughter Rosalie lived at Arlington for 84 years, dying in 1949 and bequeathing the estate to the National Trust.

Truly a globetrotter, Miss Rosalie Chichester was an inveterate collector. The charming house interior has been maintained with the original fixtures left by Miss Chichester alongside her collection of curios and model ships. I am not usually keen on swooning round the houses of dead, or for that matter living members of the aristocracy, but Arlington is a delight and well worth a visit.

Another well travelled family member, Sir Francis Chichester, Rosalie's nephew, solo circumnavigated the globe in his epic journey aboard the Gipsy Moth IV *in 1967.*

The 3500 acre estate includes a small typically Victorian formal garden with a manmade "Wilderness" to make up for the one carved up when the grounds were landscaped.

Gorgeous in summer bloom the gardens between the church and house boast shag-pile deep manicured lawns. It is a very English trait, or maybe an ingrained fear of old-fashioned park keepers, but despite there being no signs saying "Keep Off the Grass" few dared step on these formal lawns.

The stables hold a National Trust collection of some 50 carriages. Opposite its main entrance is a small early 19th century granary or cornerstone of brick and beam, moved to its present site after Dunsland House near Holsworthy burnt down in 1967.

Badgworthy Water. Photo: Walt Unsworth

On East Cleave, above Heddon (Walk 3) *(Walt Unsworth)*
Lynmouth and Foreland Point (Walk 6) *(Walt Unsworth)*

The small stone or iron herons found throughout the estate, perched on gateways and roof tops, are a motif taken from the Chichester family crest.

You will pass the algae covered "Wilderness Pond" left. The path descends cool and dark under rhododendrons, massive beech tress and with a scurrying stream for company left. Entering a dense plantation of conifers go left where the path forks, signposted "The Lake via Smallcombe Bridge". Through a gate you will enter the edge of the "Wilderness".

Another gate and you cross the bridge turning left into Woolley Wood leaving behind Arlington Court. Follow the signs to Loxhore Cott via Tuckers Bridge. In summer there is a shortcut to Loxhore Cott if you cross the river at Tuckers Bridge but the exit is closed during winter. Instead of crossing Tuckers Bridge, where there is also a small waterfall, remain right of the Yeo and climb out of the valley. The path is easy to follow and marked with yellow arrows. After a gate you are faced with a clearing but should turn left up a grassy track. At its top go left over a stile then immediately right along the hill summit ridge following the line of trees on the right. There is a fine view down the Yeo Valley and over Loxhore Cott from here.

Over a stile the easy-to-follow path enters another wood, Cott Down plantation, before leaving the Arlington Estate via a high narrow iron 'ladder' stile onto a track. At its end turn left and descend along a wide rough track to Loxhore Cott.

At the village the track becomes a road which crosses a bridge over the Yeo. On your left a small cream coloured house called Mortuary Cottage has a huge front door, presumably so that coffins could be manoeuvred back and forth.

At the next junction keep left uphill, passing a red-brick built gatehouse to Arlington Court, the entrance pillars marked with the estate's herons and snakes or eels. Uphill you will pass a set of farm buildings complete with strutting cocks - note the old AA road sign which misspells Loxhore as Luxhove.

After a short distance you have the choice of an excursion to Loxhore and the church of St. Michael or to continue directly on the return leg.

For the excursion turn left where signposted to Luxhore. A solid farm and pretty cottage is passed on the way. The Church of St.

Michael and All Saints is charming inside; particulary notable is the Norman font and its 16th century concave cover with crocketed top. The brilliance of the original paint has faded but fleurs-de-lys can still be seen.

Retracing your steps to the lane turn left, then shortly after right, following the signs to Riddle. Follow the lane past a substantial farm and Georgian house to Smythapark just before which go right, through a gate and along the bridlepath. After a ruined cottage on your right, go right. Bratton Fleming is espied across the valley into which the path descends. Through another gate you enter woodland. The path branches three ways; take the narrowest of these on the extreme right and follow the fence downhill - look for the blue arrow.

At the bottom go right over the softly plunging Yeo by a footbridge and mount the opposite valley side via a bridlepath, the foot of which is very wet even in summer. Climb directly uphill. Upon reaching a field continue to climb, bearing left to the hedge left. At the next field walk straight over - it may not be immediately apparent but, if upon reaching the wall in front you bear a few paces to the left, you will come to a stone stile part way along through the wall. Once over you are in a modern housing estate; turn left at the road and at its junction right to return to the church.

---

6. NORTH DEVON:
The remote cliffs from Lynmouth to County Gate - return via the River East Lyn - 13 miles

Directions

Start: Lynmouth, Exmoor, North Devon.

Outline and
walk length: A demanding 13 miles east along the high cliffs of North Devon. In places the route is very exposed, passing over loose scree, but a less exposed alternative is offered. Much of the path is under woodland returning via County Gate on the Devon-Somerset border and then along the right bank of the River East Lyn. Allow seven to eight hours with breaks.

Getting there:	Via the A39 or B3223.
Parking:	Car park in Lynmouth.
Refreshments:	Choice of shops, pubs and hotels in Lynmouth. Pubs in Brendon and Rockford, National Trust tea rooms at Watersmeet.
Map:	OS 1:25,000 Exmoor; Outdoor Leisure no 9.

Known as the "English Alps", Lynmouth with its associated high cliffs and deeply incised river valleys boasts some of Devon's most spectacular scenery. The area's beauty was first "discovered" during the Napoleonic Wars at the end of the 18th and beginning of the 19th centuries, when the rest of Europe was closed to the sightseers of the British aristocracy and gentry.

Since then the area has been a magnet for visitors. During its Victorian heyday paddle steamers ferried tourists to and from the beauty spots all along the North Devon and Somerset coastline.

Picturesque Lynmouth may be, but it remains haunted by the memory of a tragedy. On the night of 15-16 August 1952, 9 inches of torrential rain fell upon Exmoor in a 24 hour burst which has since been calculated at 90,000,000 tons of water. A wall of water swept down the East and West Lyn rivers killing 34, destroying 93 houses and a further 28 bridges in the area.

The scars have taken years to heal. The town had to be partially rebuilt and the surrounding woods are still recovering with the aid of careful management.

Largely composed of sessile oak, the woods have always been managed. Coppiced every 25 years or so, stout wood went off for pit props in the South Wales coal industry while the bark was used in tanning. Arriving 100 years ago you would have seen threads of smoke trailing into the sky where wood-burners were being fired to make charcoal. Many of the tracks open to walkers today are the old trails of packhorses and donkeys used to ferry the finished product out of the valley. In return for the pit props, coal from South Wales was burnt with limestone in coastal limekilns - one of which can be seen near the information centre in Lynmouth and another near Watersmeet on the River East Lyn - to produce lime with which to "sweeten" the acid moorland soil.

The cliffs are also dramatic. In some places they fall from 1000 feet to sea level in less than half a mile. Densely wooded in part, elsewhere they are

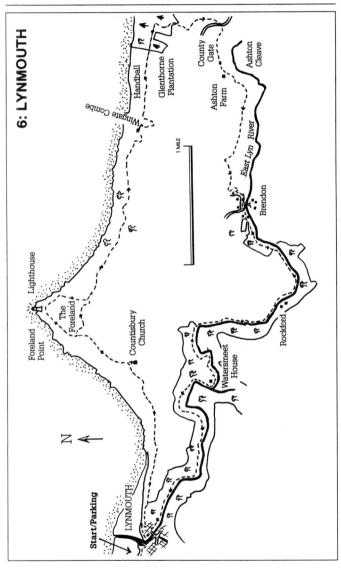

stripped of vegetation, replaced instead with sheets of loose rock or scree loosely stacked to the cliff edge.

Leave Lynmouth crossing the footbridge and following the signs east along the sea front. Passing a hotel set back from the sea wall the path bears sharp right and begins a steep switchback climb through woodland to the A39. The path follows the road for a few hundred yards uphill, either along the top of a wall or actually on the road, before bearing off left over a stile.

The line of the path can be seen ahead running round towards Foreland Point. Climbing steadily the path passes a concrete shelter, possibly linked to a cliff gun emplacement or the small disused quarry below, but otherwise it stays between the cliff and a wall enclosing the last fields this side of South Wales. Cut off the small corner where the path bears right towards Countisbury Church - it is probably wise to marshall your strength for the trials to come and so put off appreciating ecclesiastical architecture to another day.

*A coast of drama - looking back Lynmouth already seems to cower at the mouth of its river, squeezed between the sea and cliffs. Lynton, immediately inland, sits in a raised basin above the valley. At low tide a wide delta of large boulders is exposed beyond the mouth of the Lyn, testimony to the material it can move when in spate. The path curls round to Foreland Point and its now unmanned automatic lighthouse. To arrive by the exposed scree path is unbeatable (**but see below for warning**), treading your way across bare loose rock - both above and below - with the sea surging beyond. From the Point there are excellent views along the coast with Porlock clearly visible on a good day.*

Before reaching Foreland Point and its lighthouse you have a choice of routes. The coastal footpath ignores the direct approach to the Point, instead turning right and dropping down to a lane where a left turn will bring you to the lighthouse. Alternatively follow the footpath left round to Foreland Point. But beware - the path is very exposed to the elements and over loose scree. IN BAD WEATHER IT SHOULD DEFINITELY NOT BE ATTEMPTED.

From Foreland Point follow the lane back to the main coastal footpath. On the lane cross a stone bridge and walk uphill. Where the lane bears sharp right, head straight onto a track. This bears right and fades into the coastal footpath which is easy to follow

Scree on the eastern side of The Foreland

through lush, cliff clinging, deciduous woodland.

Under a moist canopy, the sea fretting out of sight, a fruiting stinkhorn decays suavely, lending lingering come-ons to woodland flies.

The path skirts in order: Coddow Combe, Chubhill Combe, Swanilcombe, Pudleepgurt and Wingate Combe. After cutting some way inland for Wingate, the last and steepest of these combes, the path drops back to the cliffs above Handball before you turn inland. Look to take the right fork, blue markered path signposted to Culbone which begins a slow climb. You will know if you are on the wrong path if it switches back on itself sharply and continues to fall - in which case retrace your steps.

The main path enters the Glenthorne Plantation of coniferous trees before emerging onto a forest track. Turn right uphill. Shortly after passing an estate house bear left off the track, shortly afterwards signposted to County Gate and Sister's Fountain. Passing the fountain or spring on the right you will emerge from the cover of trees and should turn right, signposted to County Gate and Black

Gate. After some 30 yards turn left uphill, signposted to County Gate - and the walk's summit, where you will find a walkers' shelter, an information centre and the A39 left a few wearying hours earlier on the way out of Lynmouth.

Exmoor climbs away south. Below, the East Lyn flows through flat-bottomed Ashton Cleave whose northern wall is an arid sheet of scree interspersed with small islands of bracken. The weather may be completely different with dry summery conditions along the coast replaced by moorland rain and drizzle.

Cross the car park to the viewing brass and follow the signposted path to Brendon 2 miles distant, descending gradually towards the River East Lyn. As you drop into Ashton Cleave the Brendon path ploughs on keeping a wall on the right. Look for yellow way markers where it temporarily leaves the wall below Ashton Farm. Occasionally rising but gradually turning down and heading east the path finally drops to Brendon, turning left onto a lane.

Do not cross the East Lyn by the stone bridge to enter Brendon. Instead carry on a little further, going left signposted along a track crossing a flat grassy area before running between a small smartly renovated farmstead. The path then enters the first of 4 miles of woodland accompanying the East Lyn back to Lynmouth.

The river plunges over a series of captivating waterfalls upstream of Rockford. The gloom is deep even on a bright day. For birdlife look out for the dipper, silver-backed under water, white breasted above it, and the grey wagtail bobbing from rock to rock. Sheep graze along the path and in places shoots of scree slide down to the water's edge. Watersmeet may prove an excellent and well earned watering hole before the last push to Lynmouth.

Simply stay with the path - it may twist and turn, with a few surprisingly sharp climbs, but with the river on your left as your guide you will shortly be back at Lynmouth.

---

7. NORTH DEVON:
Where Devon greets Cornwall - Hartland parish coast to Hartland Point returning via Stoke - 14 miles

---

Directions

Start: Hartland, west of Bideford and Clovelly, about 14 miles north of Bude.

Outline and walk length: A demanding walk which begins with a relatively long section of lanes before following the rugged and in places remote cliffs of North Devon. A demanding 14 miles with a number of stiff climbs. Allow eight hours.

Getting there: From the A39 trunk road turn onto the B3248 to Hartland.

Parking: Official car park with information board near the church, behind a fish and chip shop.

Refreshments: Hartland has three pubs, general stores, a cafe and a fish and chip shop. At Hartland Point there is a refreshments cabin, which may be shut out of season. Hotel at Hartland Quay.

Map: OS 1:50,000 Bude and Clovelly; Landranger no. 190.

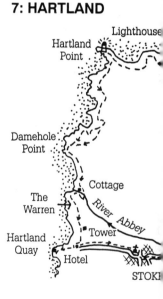

7: HARTLAND

Lighthouse

Hartland Point

Damehole Point

Cottage

The Warren

River Abbey

Hartland Quay

Tower

Hotel

STOKE

Salt burnt samphire and the bellowing Atlantic, a large ancient parish, Hartland's small fields speak of Cornwall, the Celtic fringe - it is in a sense the edge of the world.

Miles from Devon's main population centres, even in high season, Hartland escapes the multitudes, despite or maybe because of nearby Clovelly's cliff-hanging charms.

Hartland, literally "stag-island", has that slow rhythm once a feature of all Devon scarcely two decades past. A raised walkway above the road runs alongside whitewashed houses and the few shops that make up its town centre. And all the while summer's shrill piping swallows dip down the main street on swift stiletto wings.

Before setting out on the walk, or on your return, explore the church - if lucky enough to find it open - and the two potteries, as well as the small fishmonger which sells freshly caught fish from Clovelly.

Leaving the small car park, walk behind the church, turning right where you join a narrow road. This will take you past the fishmonger. As the road bends to the right, turn left down a lane leading out of Hartland. At its foot cross the small brook of the River Abbey: turn right immediately afterwards where the lane is signposted "Unsuitable for vehicles". It should be followed uphill, ignoring the

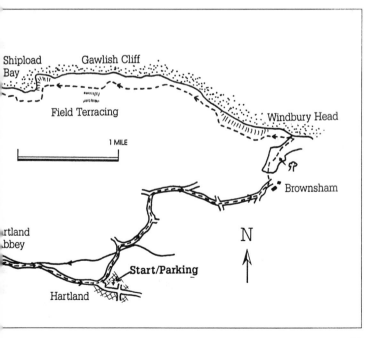

Shipload Bay

Gawlish Cliff

Field Terracing

1 MILE

Windbury Head

Brownsham

Hartland Abbey

Start/Parking

Hartland

N

farmstead of Norton, but continuing straight on until another lane is met. Turn right onto this, keeping right where it divides a couple of hundred yards along.

At the next junction cross over and follow the signs to the secluded hamlet of Brownsham.

At Brownsham enter the small car park on the left. Through the hedge on the left follow a footpath which falls into a wood sheltering in a steep combe north-west of the hamlet. Follow the National Trust permissive path and brook downstream along the left bank and near its mouth climb onto the coast path to ascend Windbury Head. This is the only very steep section of the entire walk and the route is now waymarked through fields and along the cliff edge to Hartland Point.

Geologists can have something of a field day along the cliffs to Hartland Point. From Windbury Head looking east is Blackchurch Rock, a sandwich of upstanding rock in clear bands of strata. Similarly fascinating features can be seen on the beach bed at Shipload Bay and great arches of folded strata at Hartland Point itself.

Flat-topped Lundy - literally the "isle of puffins" - broods 12 miles out to sea with all the mystery of a place tantalisingly out of reach.

On silently arched wings buzzards sail overhead, their effortless patrols only disturbed by hectoring crows or gulls. Peregrine falcons who nest along the cliffs plunge from the sky with lethal finality upon soft bodied mammals rustling the grass.

Fatacott Cliff reaches 540 feet above sea level. One dark night during the Second World War it claimed the crew of a Wellington bomber - metal, wood and bone splintering on its unyielding flanks. Their memorial and triangulation point are on the cliff summit.

At Gawlish Cliff the land has slumped idly towards the sea. Successive farmers have carved the fall into giant field terraces returning the land to production.

So to 350 feet high Hartland Point, where a slip runs down the cliff to the sea-lashed lighthouse promontory.

Up to now the walk has followed the comparatively sheltered north facing cliff - now it turns 90 degrees to face west and the full ferocity of the Atlantic. During bawling gales the sea and land wrestle and not even the now automatic lighthouse's warnings have been enough to save some ships. One, the Elisa Johanna, *lies broken backed upon the beach where she was wrecked in 1968. At low tide it is worth scrambling over the boulders to gaze at the hulk. Red-raw with rust its bowels of engine and cable hang gaunt, lifeless, its hull concussed and punctured where rammed upon the rocks.*

The beach floor is a mass of round stones larger than pebbles but smaller than boulders - they are grey but irregularly blotched with pinks and purples, glistening beautifully when wet.

From Hartland Point retrace your steps to the coastal footpath, avoiding the wooden staircase starting part way up the slipway - it is rotten and dangerous.

The route now turns south along rugged cliffs. The path is easy to follow in most places, turning a little inland and passing in front of a mobile, or in this case particularly immobile, home before climbing the opposite hillside.

At one point you have a choice of paths. Either will do but the best is on the right dropping down and running through a small valley, open at both ends to the sea. Here the cliff is a sheet of smooth, near vertical rock, being peeled away like the skin of an onion by the sea. The other path is shorter and more level: both meet at Damehole Point. From Damehole the path falls to the mouth of the River Abbey which can be crossed near a small whitewashed, slate roofed cottage. Follow the path up the "Warren" and then turning right, so down to Hartland Quay.

A return along either side of the delightfully wooded Abbey Valley is possible from the mouth of the River Abbey. But if limbs are not too weary continue along the cliffs, climbing the Warren to the ruined Tower. Hartland Abbey, rebuilt in 1779, sits athwart its slender meadows sighted inland through the Tower's imposing arch.

At Hartland Quay a quay of any description scarcely exists, long since smashed by unbridled storms blowing from Labrador across the Atlantic. Yet looking north the rugged cliff-line, abrupt inlets and canine headlands of slate, squeezed, folded and fractured, is incomparable.

In this elemental place Hartland Quay boasts a hotel, public bar and small museum dedicated to the sea and open in summer.

To return to Hartland climb from Hartland Quay. Where the road runs directly away from the cliff a footpath runs parallel to it, through fields the other side of the left hedge, to the graveyard of St. Nectan's church, in Stoke.

At 128 feet the tower is the second highest parish church tower in
Devon. A feast of interest lies within - an unrestored 15th century rood
screen, Norman font, seating for 600 on numbered pews paid for by
parishioners through a "pew rent", and a tiny, slightly bizarre church
museum in the Pope's Chamber over the north porch.

From Stoke return to Hartland about a mile distant along the
country lane.

---

8. WEST DEVON:
Buckland Monachorum - along the Rivers Walkham and Tavy - 6 miles

---

Directions

Start:	Buckland Monachorum, 4 miles south of Tavistock, West Devon.
Outline and walk length:	Across heathland with compelling views of the western flanks of Dartmoor and along the deep twisting wooded valleys of the Rivers Walkham and Tavy. A moderate walk with one climb, 6 miles in all. Allow three hours.
Parking:	In front of church.
Refreshments:	The Drake Manor Inn, and shop in Buckland Monachorum.
Map:	OS 1:50,000 Plymouth and Launceston; Landranger no. 201.

*Sir Francis Drake's buccaneering ways brought new wealth to this corner
of West Devon. A national hero he may have been but when he wasn't
robbing the Spaniards he was retiring at his family seat Buckland Abbey,
itself seized from the Church by Henry VIII upon the Dissolution of the
Monasteries, and bought by Drake in 1581.*

*Religion and the Drakes are intertwined in this corner of Devon.
Buckland Monachorum translates as "Buckland of the Monks", after the
cowled pious figures who used to inhabit the nearby abbey. Inside the
Church of St. Andrew, the walk's start, the Drake Chapel remembers the
family descended from Thomas Drake, Sir Francis' brother. The church
with its slender, high pinnacled and, as it turned out, structurally suspect*

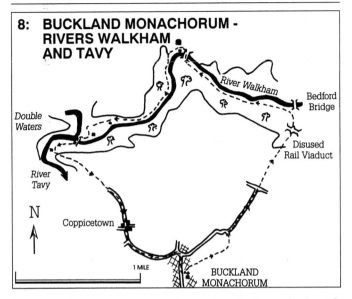

8: **BUCKLAND MONACHORUM - RIVERS WALKHAM AND TAVY**

River Walkham

Bedford Bridge

Double Waters

Disused Rail Viaduct

River Tavy

N

Coppicetown

1 MILE

BUCKLAND MONACHORUM

tower is worth taking the time to explore. Built in the Perpendicular style during the 15th century it is wagon vaulted. Its most interesting feature is the enormous "pepper-pot" late Saxon or early Norman font in the north-west corner.

To begin the walk face the church from the road and follow the path on the left skirting round the outside of the churchyard. Follow it with the church now on your right to an iron kissing gate. From here it runs up to a stone stile, over which go left across a field to another stile and then follow the hedge on your right to still another stile. The path is yellow arrow waymarked round a corrugated roofed barn which you should keep on your right while now following a hedge on the left. At the next gate there is another stone stile taking you onto a track which you should follow as it curves left to a gate leading onto a metalled lane. Turn right and walk to the end where it meets a common of heath, grass and bracken.

Looking east there are cracking views to rough edged granite grey Dartmoor, with Tavistock to the north. On leaving the lane and

45

walking onto the common look to head downhill. This will mean you taking one of the many small paths through the bracken north-east, as opposed to the wide grassy avenues which bear off north and north-west. Shortly you will find yourself in a small deepening valley. Keeping the wood on your left as you fall, a viaduct of the now disused railway to Tavistock will dominate the skyline. Pass underneath and follow a small stream - dry in summer - downhill to the car park at Bedford Bridge.

Walk through the car park towards the bridge, but turning left before it and walking downstream along the Walkham with the river on your right for a mile until you reach another bridge.

The path is well worn with tree roots running in all directions like the exposed ceiling ribs of some bizarre subterranean structure - which in a sense they are. Brown trout lie up in still pools, the woods are a chorus birdsong. Shortly you will come upon a ruined building at the level of the river. It seems to have a millrace but a waterway, possibly a leat, leads away from the Walkham and following it a short distance will bring you to the partially sealed entrance of a mine adit. A cool breeze blowing straight from its mouth, where a handful of concrete blocks have been knocked out, sends briars near its entrance swaying. Retracing your steps the path enters a clearing.

Cross the Walkham via the stone bridge to the opposite bank. Look to leave the metalled lane after a few yards left down a signposted public bridleway.

The path is now wider and grassier under mature trees running through an area of flat ground next to the river. Where the steep heavily wooded valley side meets this level area there are frequent signs of ruined buildings. Shortly you will come to a chimney some 30 feet high which gives the game away. This was copper mining territory in the 19th century. So rich were the deposits in the locality and especially those of Devon Great Consols Mine near Tavistock - which in its heyday employed 1300 - that between 1860 and 1865 over half the world's copper came from Devon.

The valley is itself very beautiful with a combination of oak, ash and silver birch. In places rough crags of bare rock overhang the path. The river slides over a series of small waterfalls and pools. At the foot of one fall a particularly deep, almost circular basin has been cut with a deeply incised and undercut lip.

After three-quarters of a mile the path climbs above a private

The Walkham downstream of Bedford Bridge

house onto a track before falling back left to the river where it rejoins the Tavy at Double Waters.

An enchanting spot. Only water, woodland and bare rock can be seen in any direction and narrowing one's eyes on a hot humid day the imagination needs little prompting to be transported to more tropical climates and scenery. It is possible to take a narrow path to the rocks at the summit of the two rivers' junction. Double Waters is a place which feels somehow magically moved from all the "busyness" of day to day life so close by.

Having drunk in the scenery cross the Walkham via a footbridge immediately upstream of where it joins the Tavy. Follow the united Tavy now on your right downstream a short way. You will cross more mine spoil heaps, this time marking the site of the Virtuous Lady Mine, reputedly first worked in the reign of Queen Elizabeth I, hence the name. As the path climbs away from the river and turns sharply left go up to the gate ahead. The building still lived in to this day used to be the mine captain's house. The path climbs and as it does so leaves the wood onto open heath.

Gradually a scene of interlocking spurs emerges, with both rivers upstream and Tavy downstream shrouded from view in their steep valleys by the dense woodland you have just emerged from. The flat valley side summits are broken into a checkerboard of small fields. Once again Dartmoor, the source of its children, the Walkham and Tavy, broods on the skyline.

Follow the track to its end where it passes through a gate onto a lane between hedges. This runs straight over a crossroads at Coppicetown - and then down to Buckland Monachorum, its church a guiding landmark should there by any doubt over your direction.

---

9. WEST DEVON:
Bere Alston - Bere Ferrers strolling the peninsula along the Tamar and Tavy - 9 miles

Directions

Start: Bere Alston, 7 miles north of Plymouth as the crow flies.

Outline and walk length: Mostly level walking with a handful of short sharp climbs

	along footpaths and lanes following the Rivers Tamar and Tavy between Bere Alston and Bere Ferrers. Some 9 miles long. Allow five hours.
Parking:	On Fore Street immediately beyond the shop-lined narrow section and in front of Holy Trinity Church.
Refreshments:	Plenty of shops including a bakery and the Edgcumbe Inn in Bere Alston. Bere Ferrers village stores and the Old Plough Inn.
Map:	OS 1:50,000 Plymouth and Launceston; Landranger no. 201.

Bere Alston has the sort of sleepy rural atmosphere which you would expect to find a good distance from a large urban area. Yet with Plymouth on the doorstep it seems remarkable to walk into the sort of village-cum-town which still supports a full range of local - and locally owned - small shops, general stores, a butcher, baker and candlestick-maker. (Well not the last one, but you get the idea.) Seven miles from Plymouth as the crow flies you would expect it to have become a dormitory town for commuters.

That this does not seem to be Bere Alston's or, for that matter, the whole of the Bere Ferrers parish's fate probably owes something to the fact that south of the A390 running into Cornwall from Tavistock only the smallest of country bridges connects the parish peninsula to the "mainland", surrounded as it is on three sides by the waters of the Tavy and Tamar.

History has yet to be subsumed under a housing estate, the condition of so much of South Devon over the last thirty years.

The names of parish farms like Whitsam, Gnatham, Rumleigh, Gawton and Barton all date from Saxon times. Nearer, if not recent history saw extensive mining of silver and lead from the 13th century onwards. Lockridge Mine, near the farm of the same name on the east bank of the Tamar, was one such site. On the orders of Edward I forced labour was used from 1295, when 340 miners from the Peak District of Derbyshire tramped for 12 days to reach the mines under penalty of death. For two hundred years mining flourished before waning, only to be revitalised at the beginning of the 19th century when steam power made mining to greater depths, including under the Tamar, possible.

So successful became the associated industry of lead smelting that the furnaces of the Tamar Smelting Works at Weir Quay received ore from Wales, Spain, France, and Newfoundland. Ships of up to 400 tons used to berth at the quay and furnaces continued smelting until closure in 1896.

49

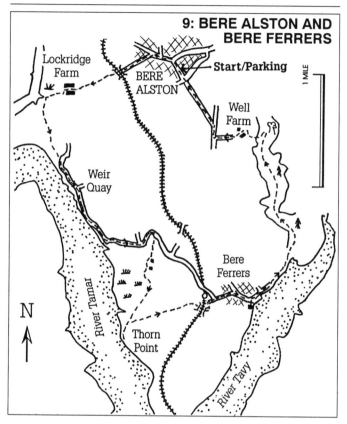

9: BERE ALSTON AND BERE FERRERS

Lockridge Farm

BERE ALSTON

Start/Parking

Well Farm

Weir Quay

1 MILE

Bere Ferrers

N

River Tamar

Thorn Point

River Tavy

Tin was also mined locally, as was copper which in the latter half of the 19th century gave the area a further boost. Associated landing quays can be seen upstream on the Cornish side of the Tamar at Cotehele.

To begin, walk through Bere Alston down the narrow, shop-lined Fore Street, carrying on downhill past the Edgcumbe Inn. Past a set of public toilets on the left the road swings right. Walk on until Lockridge Road where you turn left. You will walk through a small housing estate. The road becomes a hedge lined lane and a no through road for traffic. It passes under a railway viaduct before becoming a rough track. In front you will see the broad curve of the River Tamar.

Eventually the track falls to the rather shambolic Lockridge Farm. Walk past the farmhouse on the right and old stone barn on the left immediately past which go left to, and through a gate, then right waymarked by a yellow arrow. In keeping with the rather down at heel nature of the farm buildings there is an over-mature orchard ahead and at your back. The path now wanders downhill above a small stream entering a wood via a gate. The valley's marshy bottom is choked with tall stands of reeds.

Ignore a stile and footpath crossing the marsh right and continue ahead. The path now climbs, bearing left and south through a gate. The reed fringed Tamar is on your right and upstream Cotehele Quay can be seen. After the gate cross a small field to a stile and bear left over it. Ahead is a small copse of hawthorn. Bear left above this stand of trees, dropping down to a clearing in a tiny valley bottom. Hawthorn trees are to left and right. Now a wooden plank carries the path over the stream. Climb the steep hill facing you, going over two stiles in the process and keeping the wood and hedge on your left. Upon cresting the hill enter a lane, go left then immediately right down another signposted footpath looking south down the Tamar towards Plymouth. Keep the hedge on the left. Entering a wood owned by the Devon Wildlife Trust follow the path downhill heading south. At the path's foot a stile will take you onto a lane where you turn right.

Weir Quay is no longer the site of frantic activity. The mines exhausted, the furnaces flattened, the berth silted up, it has drifted into the history books of industrial endeavour. Now yachts sway at anchor and the occasional wind-surfer splashes by, a flash of vividly coloured sail flapping at the breeze.

Follow the road past Weir Quay and beyond where it turns inland, climbs under electricity pylons, their wires hissing malevolently like angry hornets, then falls through a tunnel of trees from which "ladders" of ivy hang. Immediately before the road bears right over a small stream, go right onto a signposted footpath under trees which crosses the stream and upon entering a field follow the hedge on the right. Keeping the hedge on your right the path goes over four stiles - salt marsh glimpsed through trees on the right. Where the path seems vague crossing an open area look for an enormous yellow arrow painted on a lone oak straight ahead. More emphatic arrows follow to ensure you do not stray from the path, guiding you to the right of a ruined farm building and then right again through an opening in the hedge facing you.

After the fourth stile the path brings you to Thorn Point and the bank (or should that be the shore?) of the Tamar.

Thorn Point is worth the diversion simply because it is the closest you will be able to walk on public ground to the apex of the Bere Ferrers' peninsula. Along the shore the Tamar is more sea than river - with the associated flotsam. Opposite is the small Cornish village of Cargreen. Walking downstream along the shore you will even come to a bare sea-cut cliff and beyond rumbling Plymouth, trains sliding over Brunel's distinctive rail bridge.

Alternatively a sharp left and the walk's main route carries you to Bere Ferrers. The path follows a fence on the right which becomes a track and finally leaves the fields via a stile. An immediate right takes you down a track under the rail line. Follow the track, then go left past the rusting parts of excavators discarded like the redundant limbs of a robot. Passing a row of houses either side, the track, now a lane, comes to a junction. Turn right and at the next junction right again, carrying you into Bere Ferrers proper.

There is no village green as such in Bere Ferrers though an open area near the Church of St. Andrew is marked by a curious grotto-type well given in 1852 by Frances Lady Shelley, "for the benefit of the poor in her son's parish." A nice thought but unlikely to improve the poor's aesthetic sense.

The church though is a gem, especially its churchyard. A notice at its entrance states: "Dogs! Please do not foul this churchyard." Smart canines indeed must bound round Bere Ferrers if they are up to reading the local ecclesiastical strictures!

The beautiful slate grave headstones hold some gorgeous names - Peter Pode, the Taperell family, William Trevail, the yeoman John German and the Luxmores. Most fascinating of all is the dedication to Thomas Lane, son of John and May who: "He, by an accident lost his life! from the bursting of the Boiler of the Queen of Calstock steamboat at North Corner, Devonport, on the 10th of July: In the Year of our Lord 1850. Aged 20 years."

Opposite the church porch one headstone simply records "CHOLERA 1849", a record of the epidemic which swept the parish in August of that year, killing 82. The disease was carried into the area by a pedlar who called in at Bere Alston. Five such gravestones in the churchyard mark the communal graves of the dead.

It is a sobering thought to consider as you gaze across the Tavy from the silent banks of Bere Ferrers.

To leave Bere Ferrers walk downhill past the Old Plough Inn and village shop to the Tavy waterfront. Walk upstream. Leave the road going right along a track running alongside the Tavy. The path follows a low bluff above the river, crosses a couple of stiles but is at all points easily followed. Before the ford at Gnatham bear left onto a track which joins a lane. Turn right along the lane. You will come to a small chalet house on your left. Go through the small blue wooden gate below the chalet entering the wood. The path climbs above a stream, under a canopy of coniferous trees. Walking upstream ignore three tempting paths on the left, especially the last which looks like the main route but is not. Keep right but do not cross the stream. Eventually the path takes a very sharp left back on itself and climbs steeply. Over a stile it enters a field. Follow the hedge round, keeping it on your left as you climb to another gate.

Go through the gate and bear right up the path, noticing Well Farm on your left. Pass through another gate then, where yellow arrowed, go left behind the older farm buildings onto a rising lane. At the next junction go right then left, leading you back to Fore Street and Bere Alston.

---

10. SOUTH DEVON:
Across the fields - Torbryan to Broadhempston - 2 miles

Directions

Start: Torbryan, between Newton Abbot and Totnes, South Devon.

Outline and walk length: A gentle country stroll with fine views, two attractive churches and no less than three pubs on the 2 mile route. Allow an hour but there are plenty of fascinating diversions to slow the walker's progress.

Gétting there: Turn off the A381 Newton Abbot-Totnes road and follow the signs to Ipplepen and Torbryan.

Parking: In village between church and Old Church House Inn.

Refreshments: Pubs - Church House Inn, Torbryan; Coppa Dolla and The Monks Retreat, Broadhempston, which has a village store.

Map: OS 1:25,000 Pathfinder series SX 86/96. The OS 1:50,000 Torbay and South Dartmoor will do but does not give much detail.

That c4ched Torbryan is on a road to nowhere in particular and is consequently a peaceful place. Visit the officially redundant 15th century Church of the Holy Trinity with its whitewashed tower and huge yew tree in the graveyard.

Described by W.G. Hoskins in his seminal work Devon *(see Bibliography) as "perhaps the most uniformly attractive church in Devon", a rather severe whitewashed tower dominates the scene. The rood screen inside dates from 1430, carved detail picked out in gold, red and green. Painted on its wooden panels are some 40 figures depicting the coronation*

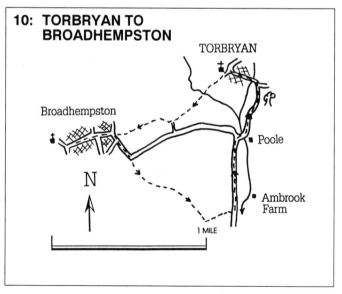

10: TORBRYAN TO BROADHEMPSTON

of the Blessed Virgin.

But perhaps the most interesting feature is the box pews. Fortunately unrenovated, scratched into them are the marks of parochial history - sometimes elegant, sometimes clumsy, the graffiti of the less attentive Sunday worshippers.

Written in a variety of hands, the graffiti can with a little effort be deciphered. Apart from the "Elsie Harris loves..." type, it includes one delightful piece which lists eleven names with the following statement:

"The Surrey XI 1888. The above named gentlemen, will have in this world plenty of cricket, and in the world to come life everlasting and still more if they behave themselves".

Whether the cricketing tourist meant this without irony, having left his mark on a church pew, remains in question!

Leaving the church, where it would be quite possible to spend a few fascinating hours, retrace your steps to the Old Church House Inn where those already exhausted by sitting in a box pew may choose to take some good quality refreshment. This is one of the walk's "rest" points which you may of course wish to visit having completed the trek's rigours rather than before.

The footpath starts just uphill of the pub and after passing through a gate follows a hedge on the left over an iron stile down to a meadow, the brook flowing through which can be crossed by a low stone slab bridge. Once over the stile through the hedge opposite, the path bears right uphill through a field freckled yellow in spring with dandelions and is waymarked by arrows on low posts.

You have to cross another stile right in the next hedge, following the path to a lane crossing via a gate into the field directly opposite. The path is again signposted and bears right across another field. A farm nestles in the combe below.

Where the path strikes the corner of the hedge turn left and over the next stile keep the brook on your right. At the next gate pass through so that the drainage ditch is on your right. At its end another stile between houses leads to Broadhempston.

Broadhempston is a village very much in the mould of Torbryan but larger. If you wish to complete the walk without a break then turn left, if not and you would like to visit another "rest" point then turn right, and the first left carries you into the main part of the village. The first "rest" is

*The white tower of Holy Trinity Church, Torbryan rises above
a village orchard*

the Coppa Dolla Inn, the second is The Monks Retreat next to the large
church of St. Peter and St. Paul. Reputedly haunted by a monk The Monks
Retreat was formerly the Church House Inn.

To return, retrace your steps to where you entered the village, walking uphill by a lane at the top of which follow the signposted footpath into the farmyard on your right, and then left round the first building up the track next to the hedge on the left. As you climb to the hill's top fine views open out. Behind is Broadhempston with hills and fields rolling towards the flanks of Dartmoor to the west, with Haytor prominent; and all around the greenery, woods and combes of South Devon.

On the left as you pass to the stile in the corner of the next field, the tower of Torbryan Church rises just out of its valley. The path runs through what looks like a recently planted beech wood to a signpost that directs you right along a hedge downhill to a gate. Here the path is waymarked. Pass through the gate and follow the field edge.

At the next gate ignore the arrow, instead keep the hedge and gulley on your right, downhill, coming out onto a lane at Ambrook Farm. Turn left onto the lane, turning right at a farm and house - marked as Poole on the map - and follow the lane and signs the short distance back to Torbryan.

---

11. SOUTH DEVON:
A short coast stroll along the mouth of the
River Dart - 4 miles

Directions

Start:	Car park near Little Dartmouth a mile south of Dartmouth and just east of Stoke Fleming.
Outline and walk length:	An easy 4 miles of track and coastal footpath walking. Allow two hours. Plenty to see including Dartmouth Castle. Some steep sections but nothing too taxing. Good going unless there is a gale from the south or west in which case low parts of the cliff path may be sea sprayed.
Getting there:	Turn off the A379 Dartmouth-Kingsbridge road, near Dartmouth and follow the signs to Little Dartmouth.
Parking:	National Trust car park at Little Dartmouth.

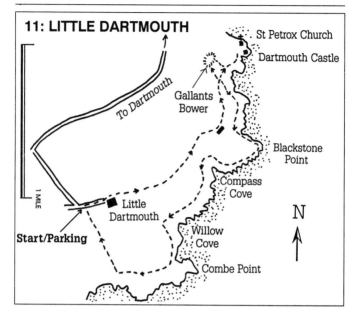

11: LITTLE DARTMOUTH

St Petrox Church

Dartmouth Castle

To Dartmouth

Gallants Bower

Blackstone Point

Compass Cove

Little Dartmouth

Start/Parking

Willow Cove

Combe Point

1 MILE

N

Refreshments: Dartmouth Castle (opening times 10am to 1pm and 2pm to 4pm throughout the year, closed Monday in winter) has a tearoom outside and toilets. Otherwise the nearest source of supplies is Dartmouth.

Map: OS 1:25,000 South Devon Outdoor Leisure no. 20.

Devon is a county with many jewels - one of its largest and brightest is Dartmouth. While this walk does not pass through Dartmouth the town can be reached via a mile-and-a-half extension from St. Petrox Church.

As a long established fishing, then commerce and now yachting centre, Dartmouth has enjoyed a diverse history reflected in its rich architecture. Violent competition for fishing and trading routes between the citizens of Dartmouth and their Breton enemies marked the 14th and 15th centuries. Such was the conflict that the king of the day would license ships and men to attack and plunder the enemy, the spoils being kept or ransomed.

During this period the forts at the mouth of the Dart were built and a chain winched between as a security measure to complement the cannon behind the stone embrasures.

Between 1600 and 1642 Dartmouth prospered with the development of the Newfoundland cod fishery. The town expanded and St. Petrox Church next to Dartmouth Castle was rebuilt. It was completed just in time for the English Civil War and for the Royalists to turn it into a store for their garrison: their effort was of little avail, however, as the fort surrendered swiftly once Dartmouth was occupied by Parliamentary troops in 1646.

Later periods saw the addition of Napoleonic and Second World War defences. So if architecture or the machinery of war is to your interest, there is plenty to see and do around Dartmouth.

Starting at the large grassy National Trust car park follow the signposted track to Little Dartmouth and Dartmouth Castle. The track leads through the farm buildings and cottages that make up Little Dartmouth then, after skirting the top edge of a grass and bracken covered field, passes a number of coastguard cottages before descending steeply to Dartmouth Castle.

Gallants Bower is a diversion worth the extra effort in which case just before you start the descent take the path left that leads to its summit. On the opposite side of the river you will be able to see the Day Beacon, and upriver commanding Dartmouth, the Royal Naval College.

You can return to the castle by a winding path due east of the earthwork. Dartmouth Castle is now owned by English Heritage, and next to it is St. Petrox Church.

The return is along the coastal footpath which, from the castle, can be reached by retracing your steps as far as Compass Cottage which almost grows out of the cliff and vegetation. Alternatively if you have reached the castle via Gallants Bower, walk uphill along the road that leads to the coastguard cottages.

At this point take the left fork in the path which is mostly level and soon runs onto the exposed outcrop of rock that is Blackstone Point.

From here you have fine views back to the forts defending the mouth of the Dart and, with a leap of the imagination, the chain that excluded marauding Bretons.

At this point the path is barely above the wave-cut platform of rock and at Compass Cove crosses a gulley, through which the sea surges, via a bridge. Keep an eye on the rocks just offshore, like Western Blackstone and Meg rocks, favourite perches for cormorants and shag.

From Compass Cove the path climbs steeply to the right and then swings left, back and higher up the cliffs. More views to the east open out across to Inner Froward Point and the Mew Stone as the path climbs round Willow Cove, below which you may see hovering a kestrel.

From Combe Point the path bears right past Warren Point which was once a commercial rabbit warren.

Here you should turn sharp right up along the track that leads directly away from the cliffs and back to the car park and start near Little Dartmouth.

---

12. SOUTH DEVON:
Far from the madding crowd -
Scabbacombe, Coleton Fishacre, and the Day Beacon - 6 miles

Directions

Start:	Scabbacombe Lane National Trust car park off the B3205 Kingswear Road.
Outline and walk length:	A South Devon coastal round between Brixham and Kingswear taking in the high cliffs of Long Sands, Coleton Fishacre house and gardens, the Mew Stone, World War II coastal defences and the Day Beacon. A hard 6 miles as the route is very much uphill and down dale. Allow four hours depending on fitness and rests. As with all cliff walks care should be taken, especially with small children.
Getting there:	From the A3022 Torquay and Paignton bypass turn onto the A379 Kingswear road. After Hillhead turn left onto the B3205, still signposted to Kingswear, and then left onto Broad Road, signposted to Boohay and Kingston. Follow the signs to Kingston, turning left onto Scabbacombe Lane before Kingston.

Parking: The first National Trust car park on the right about half a mile down Scabbacombe Lane.

Refreshments: None on walk.

Map: OS Outdoor Leisure 1:25,000 No. 20 South Devon.

Torbay hardly leaps to mind if you are a walker in search of wide open spaces and a slice of solitude. The only slice you are likely to receive in the

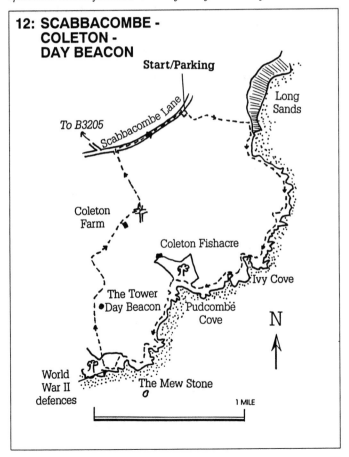

Bay is of pizza. But while the bucket and spade brigade ponder the complete disappearance of Torquay beach at high tide, the walker can find cliffs as high, wild and crowd free as anywhere in Devon, barely a mile from Brixham harbour.

The peninsula of land between the mouth of the Dart and Brixham remained in the possession of a single family who largely prohibited development, allowing the area to retain its unspoilt nature despite the frenzied holiday trade just a few miles away.

Having parked at Scabbacombe Lane NT car park (if you arrive at the entrance to Coleton Fishacre you've missed the turning), pass through the squeeze-stile and walk down the track to a larger, ladder-stile.

After the stile follow the hedge on your left downhill into a small steep valley, turning right via a lightly worn path which will bring you to the sea at Scabbacombe Sands.

From now on the walk is easy - easy on map reading though not on calf muscles. Just keep the sea on your left and walk due south and east. The path is broad and easy to follow, as it is throughout the walk.

Climb via the steps to Scabbacombe Head and Down Point. Look back to the various cliff failures and scree of Long Sands - scooped out as if by a giant ice cream scoop, and north to Sharkham Point and Berry Head.

The path runs between tall stands of bracken, curling brown and red in autumn. Look out for some particularly impressive spider's webs which stretch across the path and snap with an audible 'twang' as you walk through them.

Whining herring gulls drift by at head height, caught by the cliff up-draught, and the route becomes harder as the path twists round boulder-strewn inlets and coves.

Keep to the coast path, avoiding the temptation to shortcut back to Coleton camp and round Ivy Cove, where the angular shape of Mew Stone thrusts out of the sea, its ledges thick with nests, guano and gulls.

The path soon begins its descent to Pudcombe Cove, where the gardens of Coleton Fishacre meet the sea. The National Trust owned house and garden (open April to the end of October) was

The Day Beacon

established by Lady Dorothy D'Oyly Carte between 1925-1940.

At its foot the path meets another metalled path coming from the gardens. You either follow this to the left or walk straight over, as many walkers seem to do, under pine trees and start the climb out of the cove. At the top, benches and stone seats are provided for the weary.

By various climbs and descents the route now passes round Outer Froward Point, close to the Mew Stone, with its reeling gulls, cormorants and guillemots.

Finally, the coast path reaches Inner Froward Point, but rather than returning by the track up the right, past the Day Beacon, explore the remains of the Second World War radar station set in woodland just beyond.

The red brick barracks and radar posts are now gutted but a stepped concrete path leads down to a circular gun emplacement. Immediately above is its magazine, linked via a tram or trolley way, the tracks of which are still clearly visible. Below the concrete emplacement the path descends to two curious flat-roofed buildings. These housed searchlights which nightly lit the approaches to Dartmouth, an important naval base during the war and marshalling point for the US part of the D-Day fleet. Superb views of the Mew Stone and cliffs to the west - and a dry place for sandwiches - can be had from these wartime relics.

Once rested, return to the main path and follow the track that leads directly away from the sea past the Day Mark Navigation Beacon. A path runs across the field to the foot of the Beacon.

This Grade II listed octagonal tower is some 80 feet high, and was built in 1864 by the Dartmouth Harbour Masters who remain its owners and guardians.

Having gazed up its 'chimney', return to the track and follow it to the right, past Brownstone car park. At the track's end turn right and you will soon reach the entrance of Coleton Fishacre Gardens where you should follow the road left, past Kingston, turning right onto Scabbacombe Lane and so back to your start.

---

13. SOUTH DEVON:
The vanishing coast - Torcross, Beesands and Hallsands - 6.5 miles

Directions

Start:	Torcross at the southern end of Slapton Ley, South Devon.
Outline and walk length:	A fairly gentle coast and field round route of 6.5 miles. Allow three to four hours.
Getting there:	From Kingsbridge or Dartmouth follow the A379.
Parking:	Car park on right next to Slapton Ley immediately north of Torcross.

The River East Lyn. (Walk 6) Photo: Walt Unsworth

Refreshments: Two or three general store shops, plus a number of hotels-cum-inns at Torcross. One pub, the Cricketers Arms, at Beesands. Hotel at Hallsands providing snacks and ice creams as well as more substantial meals.

Map: OS 1:25,000 Outdoor Leisure No 20. South Devon.

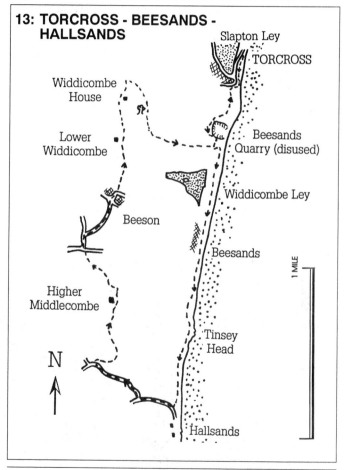

13: TORCROSS - BEESANDS - HALLSANDS

Slapton Ley

TORCROSS

Widdicombe House

Lower Widdicombe

Beesands Quarry (disused)

Beeson

Widdicombe Ley

Beesands

1 MILE

Higher Middlecombe

N

Tinsey Head

Hallsands

On the Warren above Hartland Quay. (Walk 7) Photo: Walt Unsworth

Time and tide wait for no man. One thing neither is waiting for is this part of the South Devon coast which, through the processes of erosion and deposition, they are continually shaping and reshaping - at times dramatically.

Slapton Ley, once a number of small inlets, is now separated from the sea by Slapton Sands, a shingle beach stretching for three miles north from Torcross. A similar beach deposited by the action of tide and wave encloses Widdicombe Ley at Beesands.

To give some idea of how recent, at least in geological time, Slapton Sands are, there is evidence that the Vikings sailed inland here in the 10th century to attack the settlement and castle at Slapton. A more recent invasion occurred during the Second World War when the area was evacuated to make way for thousands of American GIs in training for D-Day landings. The Sherman tank at the Ley's southern end is a solemn and imposing memorial to the hundreds of lives lost when a training exercise, Operation Tiger, went horribly wrong in the chilly waters of Start Bay.

Slapton Ley is now a nature reserve with coot, swan and great crested grebe amongst its residents. Reed smothered and silted up at its northern end, the shifting of the shingle beach was stabilised by the building of the toll road along its top in 1856.

The main focus of this walk is not Slapton Ley but the coastal path south of Torcross including Widdicombe Ley, Beesands and Hallsands. Leave the car park and head into Torcross. At the shops turn left to the sea wall. The houses facing the sea are well shuttered against the sea's depredations and the sea wall itself a necessary defence against the storms that in recent years have wreaked damage upon Torcross.

At the sea wall turn right so that you start to climb the cliffs out of Torcross. There is a hotel on your right as you do so and note the Second World War "pill-box" built into the cliff on your left.

The path weaves back and forth and provides fine views back over the Ley. Marked with yellow arrows the path runs through a gate into a field and, bearing slightly to the right, across the field to another gate. The path is then once again enclosed between hedge and wall as it skirts the disused Beesands Sunnydale slate quarry on the left.

The path soon begins its descent to Beesands, with Widdicombe Ley a miniature of Slapton on the right. Walk along Beesands seafront.

You will pass Beesands Rovers FC football pitch which slopes outrageously. A new sea wall buttressed with huge ugly rocks has recently been built between the village and the sea.

Passing the Cricketers Arms on the right, the next house has a small sign tacked inside the porch saying "Kings Arms", a legacy from when Beesands supported not one but two pubs.

There are a few small fishing boats pulled up on the shingle, but nothing like the time when the village was largely dependent upon the sea. Then boats would be drawn up the beach's length and herring were hung out to dry in the sea air.

Having walked the length of the village you will pass a thatched cottage on your right before climbing gently out of Beesands. The cliff path between it and North Hallsands is easy to follow. In some places it has had to make small diversions where part of the low cliffs have slumped a little closer to their inevitable demise. In others vegetation has arched over the path turning it into a gloomy but cool tunnel.

Following the cliff path from North Hallsands you will shortly arrive at South Hallsands, the village that has disappeared. The last ruined shells are the other side of the Hallsands Hotel. Their story is well known and the subject of the East Prawle Start Point walk, number 14.

Where the waves break upon the beach dazzling pebbles glisten, fleetingly varnished, and an idle half-hour can be spent here gathering a pocketful of memories.

The return leg to Torcross is fairly straightforward. Leave North Hallsands by the lane running away from the beach taking the first right where it forks, keeping the reeds and fish ponds on your right. Shortly you will come to a track signposted to Higher Middlecombe Farm some three-quarters of a mile away. The track is easy to follow though a small stream spills across it for some of the way, making the going decidedly damp in places.

As you climb the combe, you will also pass through a couple of gates. This track used to be a cart way and the old corpse road from Hallsands to the parish church at Stokenham.

Immediately after passing Higher Middlecombe on the left,

bear left then almost immediately right up a nettle-strewn footpath between high banks. This is the old track to the farm superceded by a later lane bulldozed during the early 1940s. At the top of the path turn right onto a lane.

Follow this lane to a junction, taking the second right which will drop you down towards Beeson past farm dogs - ubiquitous hereabouts. At the village bear right where the road forks but then keep left until you see in front a track between a number of modern houses. This becomes a footpath that follows a low stone wall, with Widdicombe Ley on the right.

The path climbs past Lower Widdicombe Farm on your left going through a gate. It runs through a field uphill, with a wood on the right crossing a couple of stiles and passing between the back of Widdicombe House on the right and a set of stables. Reaching the driveway to the house bear sharp right. You will now be walking downhill. Where the drive bears right to the house carry straight on to a gate. Turn left onto the footpath which runs parallel to Widdicombe Ley on your right and a field's edge. Over a stile rejoin the coastal footpath where a left turn will take you back to Torcross.

---

14. SOUTH DEVON:
South Hams coastal glory - East Prawle, Hallsands, Start Point - 9 miles

Directions

Start:	East Prawle, south of Kingsbridge.
Outline and walk length:	Field, lane and cliff walking, 9 miles in all. The route is rather demanding and the cliff path exposed around Start Point where extra care should be taken. Allow four hours for the walking and a couple more to enjoy the sights.
Parking:	Alongside the village green in East Prawle.
Refreshments:	A couple of pubs in East Prawle plus general store. Hotel and tea rooms at Hallsands.
Map:	OS 1:25,000 South Devon.

This stretch of the South Devon coastline was notorious for the number of shipwrecks it claimed but what was a mariner's loss was a villager's gain.

One local vicar, on hearing of a wreck while in mid service, is reputed to have leapt from the pulpit shouting to the congregation "There's a ship aground near Prawle, but let's all start fair" as he led the dash out of the church for the loot.

On November 8th 1738 a Dutch East Indiaman, De Boot, crashed onto the rocks at Prawle Point - there was no saving its cargo of porcelain but 12 boxes of uncut diamonds were passed to the shore; one was handed to a local man who took such care of it that it has not been seen since.

Rather than rushing to Prawle Point, this walk goes inland to strike the coast at the sad village of Hallsands. By following the ridges it is possible to avoid most of the steep combes which have been cut through the old cliff line - a relic left high and dry, when the sea level was up to 430 feet higher than today.

To start, leave East Prawle, passing the Pigs Nose pub on the left and follow the road round left then right, at first downhill and then uphill past a telephone box. At the top where the road turns sharply left there is a bridleway right, down which you walk.

The path is between two hedges and goes a little right then left. It descends gently before entering a field, following the hedge left and climbing to a signposted junction.

If you want a short walk turn right to Woodcombe Sand, three-quarters of a mile away: otherwise continue straight on signposted to Lannacombe Green.

Pass Woodcombe Farm, keeping the farm on your right before turning right. Follow the track uphill, a signposted bridleway, round Higher Borough Farm, through a metal gate and then into a field keeping the hedge left. Shortly you will pass through another gate: the path runs between two hedges at the end of which two tracks cross and you need to enter the opposite field so that you follow the line of the hedge which is now on your right.

From here you will have fine views north to the russet flanks of Dartmoor and Western Beacon at its southernmost end. East, a towering sky - the land and sea bit players in the meteorological show.

A number of gates follow in quick succession as the bridleway

14: EAST PRAWLE - START POINT

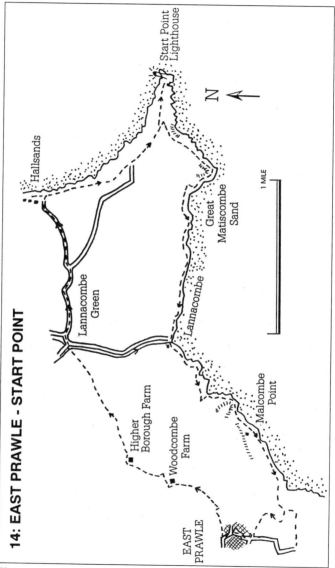

runs due east between hedges and then into a field. Eventually, marked with a blue arrow, it bears left through a gap in the hedge and goes downhill steeply.

The path bears left before passing through a gate onto a lane. Here turn right and go along a very narrow lane. You will come to a meeting of lanes scarcely worthy of the name junction. Go right, then a few yards later, left. Walk the lane uphill. At the next road junction go straight over, following the lane to its end at Hallsands.

It is worth having a break here. The Trout Hotel hosts a photographic record of Hallsands fishing village before its destruction in the Great Storm of 1917.

Its wrecking was no accident of nature. Hallsands consisted of two long rows of cottages divided by a central track. It had been built upon an ancient wave-cut platform at the foot of the cliffs. While its site seems exposed it had been protected by a long deep beach similar to the one at Beesands, now partially hidden under tons of sea defence rock.

As the 19th century waned, work began on the extension of Devonport Dockyard, Plymouth. Developers cast around for a cheap source of the gravels needed for concrete and lighted upon the huge shingle bank in Start Bay. Between 1897 and 1902 this was ruthlessly dredged despite the protestations of villagers who feared the destruction of their inshore fishing grounds. It soon became apparent though that shingle taken from the bank was being replenished by the coastal current stripping shingle from Hallsands beach. The beach level plummeted - in places by 13 feet. Hallsands' fate was sealed.

In 1903-4 storm damage ripped away much of the protective beach and later in the year part of the village pub, the London Inn, collapsed. This presaged Hallsands' final and complete destruction in the Great Storm of 1917.

Many of the villagers were subsequently rehoused immediately north of the Trout Hotel between the sea and Bickerton. Two of the original houses at Hallsands are still occupied during the summer months but each winter more of the ruins disappear and in the last three years the narrow track to them has been washed away.

Leaving this sad sight, rejoin the coastal footpath near the Trout Hotel and trace its sweep round to Start Point. In spring and early summer this section is glorious with bluebells.

At the small car park you can choose a shortcut by the footpath to Great Mattiscombe Sand, avoiding a narrow section of coastal

Old Hallsands

path round the point but also missing the lighthouse. Or you can go straight on down the asphalted road to Start Point itself. Since becoming automatic the lighthouse is sadly no longer open to the public.

Immediately offshore are the Skerries, an area yachtsmen are wise to be wary of because of the winds and strong tidal pull. Elizabethan pirates also had cause to shun Start Point. Here brigands of the high seas who fell foul of the authorities were left in chains to drown, then hung out to deter others.

From the lighthouse you must retrace your steps, going left and following the cliff path round Peartree Cove where it is rather exposed. From here back to East Prawle it is simplicity itself: follow the glorious cliff path.

The curious cliffs on your right mark an old coastline when the sea level was higher. The path weaves back and forth, past the cottage at Lannacombe. Look out to sea here and you may spot a seal - Prawle Point is one of the two sites in Devon where grey seals breed.

And so back to East Prawle which can be reached via the bridleway on the right a short way past Malcombe House, or by going "the last mile" to Devon's most southerly place, Prawle Point, and following the lane back.

---

15. SOUTH DEVON:
To Devon's southernmost place - Prawle Point, Gara Rock and Mill Bay - main walk 9 miles, two short routes both 3 miles.

Directions

Start:	East Prawle.
Outline and walk length:	A dramatic coastal circular walk. In places the cliff path is particularly exposed and extra care should be taken. The main walk is 9 miles, which will take four to five hours, depending on breaks. Short walks A and B are both 3 miles long taking two hours each at most. Moderate walking with some brisk climbs.
Getting there:	From the A379 Kingsbridge-Dartmouth road follow the signs to East Prawle from Stokenham or Chillington.
Parking:	East Prawle or, if full, Prawle Point car park. If you choose to follow route B park at the National Trust owned car park at Mill Bay.
Refreshments:	East Prawle contains one post office, a general store, a cafe, and two pubs, one of which is the most southerly in Devon. At Gara Rock there is a hotel where lunches and afternoon teas are served, and a small shop in the foyer.
Map:	OS 1:25,000 South Devon Outdoor Leisure No. 20.

Prawle Point is the most southerly place in Devon. Lashed by westerly winds during storms this jagged coastline has punctured many a ship's hull and claimed lives across the centuries. Most inland villages bear the graves of strangers wrecked upon these shores.

On December 10th 1868 the Gossamer *sank off Prawle Point. The graves of Captain John Thomson and his wife Barbara Kep, both from Rothesay on the Isle of Bute, can be found in Chivelstone churchyard. Their graves are separate from those of the villagers as if, by association in death, they bear a curse.*

Salt-burned Prawle Point is a place to suck in deep draughts of sea air. Look west. In the foreground is Gammon Head, a canine amongst the cliff's sharp incisors; beyond the coast rolls to the mouth of Salcombe Harbour. Looking east is Start Point. You may wonder why there are cliffs not only where the land crumbles into the sea but also at different levels, like a

73

staircase climbing inland. These outcrops were cut during warmer spells many millions of years ago, when the sea was at different levels - at one point 430 feet higher than at present.

The return leg of the main walk - and short walk A - runs at the foot of this relic cliff.

The present-day earth and boulder 'cliffs' to the east are the remains of the soil and rock which slipped down from the cliffs above during the seasonal periglacial freeze-thaw periods of the last glaciation 10,000 years ago.

Leave East Prawle, an unpretentious South Hams village, and follow the road towards the sea. After bearing right downhill, the road takes in quick succession a left then a right, where a footpath leading to the cliff is signposted on the left through a gate.

The path wanders along next to a field of wheat before joining the coastal footpath, where you turn right towards the sharp outcrop of Prawle Point to which you climb.

Notice to your right and ahead three grass and bracken-covered mounds. These are not prehistoric barrows but the remains of a Second World War radio station. The iron hooks set in concrete around them used to be the tying points for camouflage netting. The last bunker before the climb to Prawle Point is now a cattle shelter and, for those who can stand the smell, can be explored.

Having climbed Prawle Point the path descends passing through a row of upright stone slabs, an example of a prehistoric field boundary or "orthostat" wall. Below lie the rusting remains of the Demetrios, *a cargo ship which, under tow to the breakers, broke free of its tug during a storm in December 1992. Its back snapped and now each winter the sea dismantles it some more.*

Leave Prawle Point and descend. The path curves back upon itself towards Gammon Head where the sea boils over rocks into narrow clefts. After Gammon Head, a glorious prospect opens out to the mouth of Salcombe Estuary, and the path winds around, clinging to the cliff's side.

During spring and summer, flowers make the path a celebration of colour. You may also find what appear to be thin strips of brown deep-pile carpet on the move, which on closer inspection turn out to be hairy caterpillars. If you stumble over a party living it up on the foliage then the collective term locally is a "rug".

A story is told of one local inebriate who returned home one star-lit summer's night a little worse for wear from his favourite hostelry. His wife, none too pleased, had barred the front door and the local ne'er-do-well was faced with a chilly night slumped in the porch. So he was almost overjoyed when he found a warming blanket, which he presumed his wife had thrown out for him, immediately prior to his banishment.

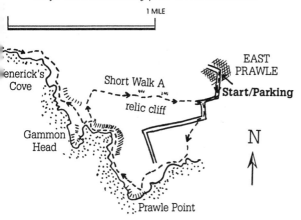

15: PRAWLE POINT

He slept soundly but woke at dawn's first blush to find to his astonishment the porch a soundless arching of butterfly wings and his blanket gone.

Another half an hour or so should bring you to Gara Rock and its sandy, gently shelving beach. This is a popular bathing spot for those who enjoy sea temperatures that in a good year flatter the sub-arctic.

After a rest - and for swimmers, resuscitation - the path climbs to Gara Rock Hotel and then descends back to the cliff edge as it runs along Portlemouth Down. Here the "pebble-tapping" red throated stonechat can be seen atop spikes of gorse.

Now the path bends into Salcombe Estuary. Across the water lie the ruins of Salcombe Castle, the last fort in Devon to hold out for Charles I during the Civil War. Shortly the path runs into woods and down to Mill Bay, a popular family beach where there are toilets, and the National Trust car park from which walk B starts.

Here leave the South Devon coastal footpath you have followed since Prawle Point to follow an ordinary yellow arrowed track gently uphill. The path has a little right 'kink', where it passes through a gate and runs up over a stile, through a field. At its end is another stile after which you turn right, which brings you back to Gara Rock Hotel.

This is the halfwayish point for those on walk B who, after visiting the unusual thatched coastguard lookout post, follow the Portlemouth Down section of the coast path.

The main walk now returns along the coast to Gammon Head. Before starting, look opposite to Deckler's Cliff where, with the sun behind you, you are able to pick out the old field system. Once back at Gammon Head take the path sharp left and directly uphill, marked "Circular Walk", which is also the return for those walkers following walk A.

After turning hard right near the hill's top, the track runs at the foot of the relic cliff mentioned earlier. East Prawle is now just a few gasps away.

---

16. SOUTH DEVON:
Where the Armada landed - Bigbury-on-Sea to Kingston and Ringmore - 9 miles

---

Directions

Start: Bigbury-on-Sea, south-west of Kingsbridge.

Outline and
walk length: A 9 mile round along the South Devon coastal footpath. A
                  number of steep climbs and descents on the coastal sec-
                  tion. Allow four to six hours depending on fitness and
                  breaks. Add half an hour if you visit Burgh Island - rather

longer if you get cut off by the tide.

Getting there: From the A379 Plymouth-Kingsbridge road take the B3392 and follow the signs to Bigbury-on-Sea.

Parking: Paying car park for Burgh Island at Bigbury-on-Sea.

Refreshments: Bigbury-on-Sea and Challaborough, the usual seaside ice cream vendors. Also pubs: the Pilchard Inn on Burgh Island, the Dolphin Inn at Kingston and the Journey's End at Ringmore.

Map: OS 1:25,000 Newton Ferrers and Thurlestone, Pathfinder 1362. An OS 1:50,000 Torbay and South Dartmoor would do but it may not show the footpath running across the fields from Kingston to Ringmore.

Smugglers laced their way through the creeks of South Devon for hundreds of years. Smoky walled taverns heard the hatching of their "rum and 'baccy plots". One such was the 14th century Pilchard Inn on Burgh Island across from Bigbury-on-Sea. If the tide is out it is worth a short stroll over the golden sands to visit the island. The Pilchard Inn is not the only interest - the 1920s-built hotel was a favoured haunt of Agatha Christie. A small stone building at the island's summit is a former tea house frequented by the gentry during the last century. From here looking west you will be able to see the length of the walk's coastal section to the mouth of the River Erme, cliffs glinting silver in the sun.

Of course if the tide is in you will miss all this. But a reminder of the area's smuggling days can be had in the name of the Tom Crockern Bar at the end of the car park. Tom was a local smuggler shot by an Elizabethan (Elizabeth I that is) customs officer. Now his name graces the bar, the iron girders of its exterior weeping rust, and where the smell of chips may be overlaid with the sound of country and western music oozing from the juke box inside.

Follow the path behind the Tom Crockern Bar. This path runs along the road in front of a number of houses, turns right and is signposted as a track down to Challaborough.

Once a clutch of fishing cottages Challaborough has been surrendered to a tribe of caravan trailers. This is your last call to stock up on ice cream. Walk along the road that runs parallel to the beach and up the path which climbs the cliffs, turning left at the slipway. Ahead is the first of at least four ascents. Each offers, apart

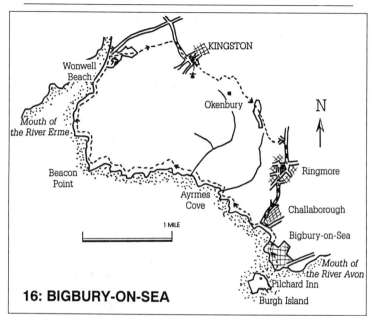

Wonwell Beach

KINGSTON

Mouth of the River Erme

Okenbury

N

Beacon Point

Ayrmes Cove

Ringmore

1 MILE

Challaborough

Bigbury-on-Sea

Mouth of the River Avon

16: BIGBURY-ON-SEA

Pilchard Inn

Burgh Island

from exhaustion, views back to Burgh Island and the mouth of the River Avon.

The path runs close to the cliff in places - so caution should be exercised - and crosses streams flowing from tight miniature valleys by a series of wooden footbridges. In some places it is possible to see where great slabs of shale folded on end are being peeled away by the insidious effort of seawater and salt squeezed into the fissures.

After what seem like too many ups and too few downs the footpath curves round to reveal the sandy mouth of the River Erme.

Looking north Dartmoor broods in its browns, yellows and purples - last out of winter, first into autumn. The Erme is a great play area when the tide is out - drivers unleash their labradors, kites fly, and children squeal or wail depending upon their mood. And when the hawthorn, bearded with lichen, blossoms, it lends a heady musk to the air.

After a gentle climb the path descends into woodland almost level with Wonwell Beach and down a few steps to the end of a road. Walk along the road, turning right after some 50 yards up a signposted footpath which once again enters the woods. It climbs steadily through the wood which is carpeted in bluebells during spring. The path drops down left over a couple of "knuckles" of ground before bearing right and continuing its climb. Eventually it levels out alongside the edge of a field before ending at a stile. Cross the stile into a field where you follow the hedge on the right, then over another stile between two hedges, over another stile, and across a second field.

Look north to a russet Dartmoor, the central cleft where the River Erme escapes its sustaining bogs. Rising above it are Butterdon Hill, Ugborough Moor, Stalldown Barrow, and to the west Penn Beacon.

Once across the field, through a gate turn right onto the lane that leads to Kingston.

At the crossroads turn left passing the 14th century church of St. James the Less, and then right "through" the Dolphin Inn, which straddles the road and which also boasts wood of an Armada galleon inside.

At the next junction a left will take you into the main body of the village. Instead turn right uphill then first left signed as a dead end. The short lane becomes a track; where it forks keep left. A bridlepath leads ahead; instead turn left where signposted and the path goes diagonally through a field and newly planted orchard.

It is this path between Kingston and Ringmore that is not marked on the OS 1:50,000 Torbay map and it skirts fields following the hedge left, making four sharp turns as it does so before crossing a lane, to the right of which is Okenbury. The path now runs to the stile opposite. There are views seaward as you follow the hedge left, to a stile. Once over, the path crosses another field to a stile on the edge of a wood. The path slips steadily downhill to a pair of ruined buildings, Noddonmill, in the valley bottom, before climbing a short way by a wide track. Near its top the path bears right over a stile.

Follow the path along another track via a gate through a field, bearing right to another gate. In front you will now see Ringmore and its church. Cross to the left-hand corner of the field, passing over two stiles and another field, joining a lane next to a high wall. Turn right into the village, and right again following the signs back to Challaborough by road and the footpath to Bigbury-on-Sea. And, who knows, maybe the ice cream kiosks will still be open.

---

17. SOUTH DEVON:
Wild and spectacular - Outer Hope, Bolt Head and Bolt Tail - 11 miles

---

Directions

Start: Outer Hope, near Kingsbridge.

Outline and
walk length: From Outer Hope to Overbecks and back via Bolt Head and Tail is 11 miles over some of the wildest, most spectacular coastline in Devon. It includes strenuous climbs along the cliff section and six hours should be allowed, longer if you intend to visit Overbecks. Alternatively a shorter route of 4.5 miles is possible returning to Hope Cove from Bolberry Down along the cliffs.

Getting there: From Kingsbridge follow the A381 towards Salcombe turning off right and following the signs to Outer Hope.

Parking: Car park at Outer Hope.

Refreshments: Pub and small hotel at Hope Cove, also the Port Light Hotel on Bolberry Down - otherwise carry the rations you will need.

Map: OS 1:50,000 Torbay and South Dartmoor area. The National Trust leaflet 'Salcombe (West)' includes a map and would be an asset.

It was an early bawling wind and sea-lashed September day when I first set out to walk the spectacular cliffs between Bolt Head and Bolt Tail. For mariners these cliffs are some of the most dangerous in Britain, claiming 40 vessels between 1700 and 1972. Hope Cove was the site in 1588 of the only Armada galleon to be shipwrecked in the whole of England. Having been driven round Scotland and Ireland by storms its exhausted crew were in no fit state to fight the final westerly that drove them ashore, 140 of those aboard surviving.

Hope Cove the village is comprised of Inner and Outer Hope. From the car park a footpath runs along the seafront to Inner Hope, in which case you will pass the tiny church of St. Clement's on your left, once the village school. Alternatively, if the car park is full and you have to park a little further away, make your way by the road,

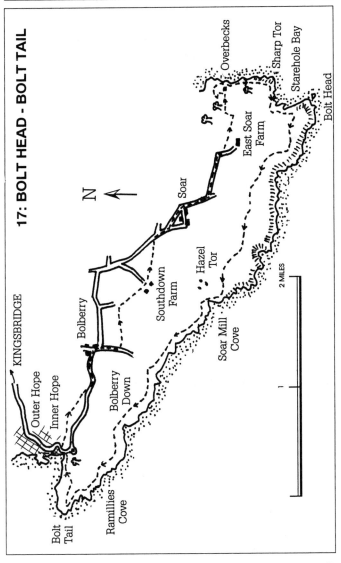

17: BOLT HEAD - BOLT TAIL

N

KINGSBRIDGE

Outer Hope
Inner Hope

Bolberry

Bolberry
Down

Southdown
Farm

Soar

Hazel
Tor

East Soar
Farm

Overbecks

Sharp Tor

Starehole Bay

Bolt Head

Soar Mill
Cove

Ramillies
Cove

Bolt
Tail

2 MILES

1

in which case the church will be on your right.

Hope Cove is protected by a low sea wall and shelters under deep red sandstone cliffs. At the time of my visit there was a village festival. The beach divided into squares was being dug frenziedly by 'treasure' hunters. Round at Inner Hope hardy visitors braved an overcast sky determined to enjoy their day. Offspring despatched to the sea quickly took on a grey shade of blue while parents wrestled with recalcitrant deck chairs. Inner Hope is a lovely thatched square of cottages, once known for its smugglers and crabs - though not crab smugglers. Nowadays it is more notable for its holiday lets and executive cars.

Having put your head round the square retrace your steps a little to the yellow/beige thatched cottage set immediately back from the sea wall. With the sea at your back face the cottage and walk along the path on its left. Follow it going through the right gate of two, and then straight on through another and onto National Trust land and a permissive path. Follow the brook and bear right up to a ladder-stile. Hope Barton Farm is on your left but you need to go straight uphill on the public road towards Bolberry. At Bolberry House Farm the road bears right, so that the farm is on your left.

At the next junction turn right uphill signposted towards Bolberry Down, half a mile away. The hill is fairly steep and near the top, before the transmitter, go left along Jacob's Lane footpath.

For those wanting a shorter walk head straight on to Bolberry Down and turn right at the cliffs back towards Hope Cove.

Jacob's Lane is narrow and stickily muddy. At the first stile on the right, turn right and follow the edge of the hedge right. This brings you to the outbuildings of Southdown Farm where you bear left.

At the road cross over, follow the hedge right to the gap and then bear diagonally left across the field. This is not signposted though there was a worn narrow path through stubble at the time of walking. You are here on a wide open ridge with views back to the sea, inland to the spire of Malborough Church and looking north the southern flanks of Dartmoor, a sombre companion for iron-clad skies. At the next gap in the hedge the path again goes across the fields to a stile that brings you onto a lane where you should turn right, uphill, signposted to Soar. Where it forks keep left, ie. not to

Soar Mill Cove. Follow the road round passing on the right a row of white-painted, slate roofed houses. Keep straight on up to the National Trust car park where upon entering you should go left, skirting the site of a Second World War airfield. The track bears a little to the right, after which there is a stile left. Cross the stile onto the Trust permissive footpath signposted to Salcombe and the YHA. Keep the hedge right, over another stile and to a combination of stiles where you should go left signposted to South Sands via Torwoods. At the next signpost go right, as the Salcombe estuary comes into view. Follow the path downhill, eventually bearing left to Overbecks.

The National Trust owned gardens and museum of Overbecks is open to the public: the garden all year, and the museum, with its bygones and photographs connected with local shipping, until October but not on Saturdays. The gardens contain some rare plants and shrubs, thriving thanks to the mild climate, and fine views to Prawle Point. Overbecks marks roughly the halfway stage before the excitement of the cliffs.

Leave the gardens, walking downhill as the road curves back on itself. Towards the bottom turn right down a track which soon becomes the Courtenay Walk part of the coastal footpath which you should follow back to Bolt Tail.

The path clings to the cliff of Sharp Tor with a guide rail to protect walkers. It skirts Starehole Bay, where on a still day the skeleton of the Finnish barque **Herzogin Cecilie** *can be made out under the water.*

At Bolt Head the path turns away within a mini valley, the remains of a coastguard lookout post at its seaward end. Keeping to the cliff it crosses The Warren, gorse clad. Note the Old Admiralty Signal Station.

The path falls to Soar Mill Cove, where as I tramped through a westerly gale the sea howled like a crying, roaring beast. The vessel-wrecking Ham Stone is offshore. Bedraggled gulls attempting to land were tossed like rags by the storm.

Looking inland Hazel Tor marks an older cliff when sea levels were higher than today - a visual note of what might happen if global warming continues without check.

Climb Cathole Cliff before walking over Bolberry Down. Port Light Hotel on the right used to be the officers' mess when the Down was the site of a Second World War airfield.

The red-throated stonechat clicks its "stone-tapping" call, perched on the upright slabs of mica-schist set on end to mark ancient field boundaries.

Just offshore from the plunging gash of Ramillies Cove is the Greystone. Here the Blesk had its bottom torn open in December 1896. Its cargo of 3180 tons of petrol spread along the coast to become the first reported case of coastal oil pollution.

As you approach Bolt Tail you will pass over the still impressive ramparts of an Iron Age fortification. Then onto Bolt Tail where the full force of the westerlies can be appreciated. The views are wonderful. The faint little finger of the Eddystone Lighthouse is in the distance while nearer Burgh Island and the silver cliffs of Bigbury can all be seen.

To return to Hope Cove follow the path round Bolt Tail which crosses the rampart, enters a small wood and keeping left you will come out once again at Inner Hope.

---

18. EAST DEVON:
High cliffs and donkeys - Salcombe Hill, Slade Farm Donkey Sanctuary and Salcombe Regis - 5 miles

Directions

Start:	Salcombe Hill immediately east of Sidmouth.
Outline and walk length:	A short coast walk along the red cliffs of East Devon taking in the Donkey Sanctuary at Slade Farm and the pretty village of Salcombe Regis. Just over 5 miles long with one stiff hill to climb. Allow two to three hours depending on stay at the Donkey Sanctuary.
Getting there:	Turn off the A3052 north of Sidmouth at Sidford for Sidcliffe, then left signposted uphill to Salcombe Regis. As the road straightens and levels out the car park is on your right.
Parking:	National Trust car park on Salcombe Hill.
Refreshments:	At Slade Farm Donkey Sanctuary, vending machine only.
Map:	OS 1:50,000 Exeter and Sidmouth; Landranger no. 192.

The landscape of East Devon with its 500 foot high plateau and steep valleys is both distinctive and dramatic, owing more in character to Dorset than the rest of the county.

Salcombe Hill commands a fine view over Regency and Georgian Sidmouth, Devon's most genteel resort. The hill's prominence also made it the favoured site of the Observatory founded in 1912 by Sir Norman Lockyer, the discoverer of helium gas. The 5 acre site opposite the National Trust car park is open to the public on Sundays between July and the beginning of September. At other times you might like to set your watches against the Analemmatic Sundial in the grounds. The correct time can be read from the fall of your shadow, as long as you stand on the right date spot on the slate slab.

Leave the car park by the gate behind the information board, turning left onto the metalled road which passes in front of a house leading to the cliffs and coastal footpath. Turn left to a viewing point and gate. Look west to Sidmouth set in a smart formal white, with Peak Hill its backdrop and Ladram Bay beyond.

Turning east with the sea and well-fenced cliffs on your right pass over Salcombe Hill and begin the knee jarring descent to Salcombe Mouth. Mount the valley side opposite following the edge of Dunscombe Cliff. The path curves left then sharp right

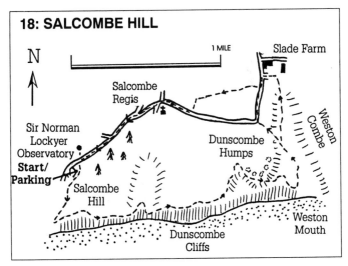

18: SALCOMBE HILL

passing as it does so a number of exposed piles of flint. This is Dunscombe Humps. After curving back to the cliff's edge the path falls in a winding manner to Weston Mouth, through a small wood rank with ivy creepers and dripping undergrowth.

So soon into a walk I always find the stiff climb from Salcombe Mouth gruelling. Down below a small fishing boat putters by, taking the easy route on its way to Beer.

At Dunscombe Humps chalk was burnt to make lime until 1906. All that remain today are the piles of burnt flints, which clink with a delightful glassy sound when walked over.

Western Combe clearly shows the different layers of rock which make up the distinctive East Devon scenery. Hill tops are clay with flints and, like the bottom layer of red Triassic Keuper marl, are fertile and well farmed. Between these two is a layer of Cretaceous greensand and chalk which being both steep and of low fertility is of little agricultural use. In Weston Combe this can be clearly seen where the steep valley sides are covered in rough bracken and scrub. At 520 feet high Weston Cliff is the highest on the East and South Devon coast.

From Weston Mouth the route turns inland, away from the geology lesson and along the western side of the valley towards the Donkey Sanctuary at Slade Farm.

Either follow a broad track through a collection of mobile homes via a lane to Slade Farm or alternatively follow the path as marked on the map. Just before the track passes under trees there is a footpath right which follows a hedge on its right, at first slightly downhill but then climbing directly out of Weston Combe - if you see donkeys then you are going the right way.

Entrance to the Donkey Sanctuary, the animals, and information centre is free - quite a rarity for Devon, a county dependent on the holiday trade and devoted to the lightening of wallets.

Established in 1969 by Dr Elisabeth Svendsen, the sanctuary moved to Slade Farm in 1974. The charity now owns nine such farms in England and Ireland. It rescues and cares for maltreated donkeys from across the globe. Through a separate charity devoted to the therapy of physically and mentally handicapped children, youngsters work with, tend and ride some of these self-same donkeys.

After exploring the Sanctuary return to the walk via the car park where a sign warns of the danger of "feeding fingers to donkeys".

Leave the main entrance, turn left down the lane for barely 50 yards before turning right onto a footpath that, running alongside a field and hedge, leads to Salcombe Regis.

There are a number of stiles to cross but the path is well signposted. Having run for less than a mile the footpath turns left round the edge of a field and rejoins the road.

At the road turn right into Salcombe Regis.

The Church of St. Mary and St. Peter in Salcombe Regis is a glory built in Beer Stone. It is at its most gorgeous in early morning or late evening sunlight. Built on the 1000 year old site of a wooden chapel to St. Clement, the church contains 12th century stained glass and a beautiful gold, dark green and red painted nave. The churchyard must be one of the most attractive in Devon, a springtime delight carpeted in daffodils and the blossom of a spreading cherry tree. Earlier this century the parish vicar was renowned for riding to neighbouring villages on horseback - with his wife and large family trailing behind on foot.

Leave the church to return to the lane junction and turn left uphill signposted to Sidmouth. At the next junction keep left along the road which leads back to the Observatory and car park.

---

19. EAST DEVON:
Across the heathland of Woodbury Common - 5.5 miles

Directions

Start:	Woodbury.Common, east of Exeter, East Devon.
Outline and walk length:	An undemanding 5.5 miles along tracks, mostly over open heathland taking two to three hours.
Getting there:	One mile east of Woodbury village where the B3179 joins the B3180.
Parking:	At Four Firs crossroads, the junction of the B3179 with the B3180.
Refreshments:	None on walk. Try Woodbury and East Budleigh for pubs, tea rooms and general stores.
Map:	OS 1:50,000 Exeter and Sidmouth; Landranger no. 192 or 1:25,000 Sidmouth.

The heath that cloaks the commons of Colaton Raleigh, Woodbury, Bicton and East Budleigh owes its existence to the sandy pebble beds below, through which moisture drains so readily. The resulting soil is poor in nutrients but excellent in visual appeal, with purple heather, blooming gorse and the greens, browns and withered yellows of grasses.

Rising to 560 feet at Woodbury Castle it is the first 'high' ground east of Exeter. It provides splendid views over the city and across to the Haldon Hills, with glimpses of the bold flanks of Dartmoor beyond.

Leaving Four Firs car park, walk due south along a broad track passing between two rectangular plantations of pines. It is slightly uphill to the trees, but thereafter the dusty, gravelly path falls left of Blackhill Quarry. Here the pebble beds, locked in a red sand, are some 103 feet thick and are dug away for use as aggregates by the road and construction industry. A sign warning of the danger of the flooded workings has been peppered with gunshot.

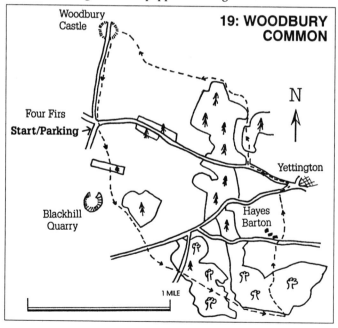

The path rises gently as you pass the quarry, and to your left there is a mixture of heath, and Scots pines which were planted out in the 18th century but now look a perfect complement to the landscape.

Pass through a small car park under the trees, and cross the road into another car park opposite, bearing left down another broad track, its entrance protected from over-eager off-road motorists by a chained log.

Within a quarter of a mile the track crosses another road and car park continuing broadly in a straight line. Keep the plantation on your left. Soon after, the path descends. Take first the left fork and then the right.

Ahead you will see a low, flat-topped, bracken-clad hill. Aim for this along a track, keeping the hill to your right, with a plantation of fir trees on the left. You are now on a sunken 'green' lane and, arrowed left, the path soon climbs a muddy track between stands of fir trees. Here the path is marked left and right with firm signs warning of dire consequences should you stray from its course.

After entering the gloom of a mature stand of fir the track leads out to open fields and past a lone cottage, your passage announced by the enraged yapping of a kennelled terrier.

Follow the metalled track to the lane. Hundreds of pigs grunt in the mire of a neighbouring field. The farm ahead left is Hayes Barton, birthplace of Sir Walter Raleigh.

Crossing the lane there is a stile almost directly opposite and you are led around the next field with an electric fence and huge boars for company. This arrangement is fine until you have to cross an opening between two fields which, with the passage of pigs, has been churned into an indescribable slurry - look for the blocks of wood for steps.

The signposted footpath rises along the edge of a couple of fields, and switches to either side of the hedge keeping it first right then left, and via another stile or two, on your right again. At a final stile, cross onto the lane, turning right into Yettington, and then immediately left, on to a busier lane, where children should be kept close to the verge.

The lane rises gently back towards the common returning directly to Four Firs crossroads. Instead, after about a quarter of a mile out of Yettington turn right down a track at 90 degrees to the lane, just before a wood.

The track - here a bridlepath - runs through a plantation and out into an area of young trees where one afternoon I found myself amid beaters, frenzied springer spaniels and men with shotguns. I rooted for the pheasants. The track turns fairly sharply left and climbs out onto the open common.

Strike off for Woodbury Castle - a prehistoric fort - up a very wide track, returning to Four Firs by a path that runs almost parallel to the road going south from the castle.

---

20. EAST DEVON:
The rounded hills north of Sidmouth - Harpford, Beacon Hill and Tipton St. John - 6 miles

---

Directions

Start:	Station Road, Newton Poppleford.
Outline and walk length:	A little over 6 miles of wood and field footpath with some lane walking. Allow three hours.
Parking:	Free car park in Newton Poppleford or on the side of Station Road which is the last road on the left as you leave Newton Poppleford going east on the A3052.
Refreshments:	Pubs and shops in Newton Poppleford. Pub and general store in Tipton St. John.
Map:	OS 1:50,000 Exeter and Sidmouth; Landranger no. 192.

Darting late summer swallows dip along the banks of the languid Otter, stoking up on insects for their long migration. The walk is dominated by the bluff, rounded greensand hills above Sidmouth. Beautifully shaped they look as if a potter had begun moulding the clay of the land only to be called away from his wheel, leaving them half formed.

The Normans had a strong say in this area's administration. The parish of Harpford centred on the Church of St. Gregory was granted to the great abbey of Mont St. Michel in 1205.

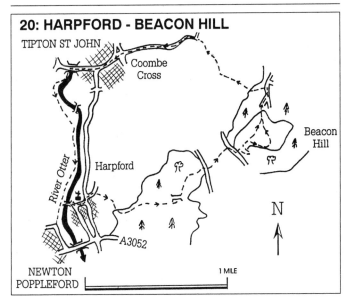

20: HARPFORD - BEACON HILL

TIPTON ST JOHN

Coombe
Cross

River Otter

Harpford

Beacon
Hill

N

A3052

NEWTON
POPPLEFORD

1 MILE

The walk follows the unhurried River Otter and for part of the way the course of a disused railway line. It starts from the footpath on the right just past the playground on Station Road, Newton Poppleford.

The river is on your right as you walk upstream. Having crossed a stile you will come to and should cross an iron footbridge over the Otter leading to Harpford Cross. At the lane turn left up to the Church of St. Gregory - heavily 'renovated' by the Victorians.

At the top of the road go left (though it is worth turning right to look briefly at a clutch of fine thatched cottages) then almost immediately go right up Knapp Lane. Part way up, the lane becomes sunken between sandstone walls. Near its top go right down the footpath signposted to Bowd. The track is waymarked with yellow arrows and part of the East Devon Way. Once over a stile the track enters a fairly open stand of pine trees. Carry straight on.

The heady tang of sticky resined pine logs filled the air on the summer's day I walked this way. Even under the cool plantation insect life hummed. A long narrow tunnel under the rail embankment of the disused Sidmouth branch line offered the temptation of a crawl to some magical, imaginary

91

world on the other side.

Look nearby for a small stream. Dry in summer it is cut deep into the sandstone and has a deep, sandy bottomed plunge pool which must make for a thunderous small waterfall in spate.

Shortly after the embankment tunnel and waterfall the path branches and you should take the left fork uphill and under an old railway bridge following the path straight on.

It climbs through a small richly-wooded valley before becoming a broad grassy track with pine trees left and open ground right. Again the path branches but keep right up to the road, crossing via a couple of stiles into the field opposite signposted "Fire Beacon".

Next follows the only real climb of the entire walk through the grassy field. Keep left where there is a gap in the metal fence and then bear right. Aim for the trees and hedge in which there is a stile followed by a flight of steps and another stile leading out onto a lane.

At the lane go right then left uphill, signposted as part of the East Devon Way. Part way up the path divides, but either way you will soon find yourself upon the summit of Beacon Hill.

At 735 feet Beacon Hill commands wonderful views south over the gently scalloped valley - Sidmouth at its mouth, west to the heathland of Woodbury Common, the Haldon Hills and on a clear day Dartmoor. The top of Beacon Hill is level, sandy-soiled, covered with heather and gorse. It supports the birdlife of heath - like the vivid yellowhammer - and underfoot scurrying lizards, and sliding by the diamond-backed adder.

A number of paths cross Beacon Hill's top, the best one skirting its edge south and east so that Sidmouth is always in view before turning left onto a track.

There is a more direct route across the summit which leaves the top by a similar track edged by vast beech trees, huge branches bifurcating from each trunk's base.

Where both these tracks join you should keep straight on through the coniferous plantation and look for a low mileage stone on your left, where you turn left.

The path falls a small way and joins another. Turn left, though not before pausing at another viewpoint with views over a patina of East Devon fields.

The path runs along the side of the hill to a lone house where it turns right sharply downhill between hedges, crosses a lane and continues to fall, bearing right at one stage and then descending all the time between hedges before bearing right and running out onto a lane. Turn left and walk downhill through the scattering of houses and farm that constitute Coombe.

At the Coombe Cross road junction go straight over into Tipton St. John, noticing left the water wheel set into a house as a window. Do not turn left but keep going downhill and you will pass the Golden Lion Inn.

Cross the River Otter by the road bridge and turn left through a gate and signposted footpath. The last mile is along the Otter on your left.

Soon the path drops right down to the river where the path has been eroded. It is just possible that if the river is full getting round here may prove difficult.

Once again the path crosses the disused Sidmouth railway line before following the serene Otter back to Newton Poppleford.

---

21. EAST DEVON:
Where the Otter lazes - Otterton to the red rocks of Ladram Bay - 6.5 miles

---

Directions

Start: Otterton is a pretty thatched village between Budleigh Salterton and Sidmouth.

Outline and
walk length: A 6.5 mile walk with plenty of excellent bird-watching opportunities along the River Otter and the red cliffs of East Devon. Allow three hours.

Getting there: From the A3052 to Newton Poppleford turning onto the B3178 then as signposted.

Parking: Along Otterton main street.

Refreshments: Otterton contains one general store and one pub as well as Otterton Mill, restaurant and gallery. On the walk there is nothing until Ladram Bay where there are ice cream stalls, and a bar selling "traditional" seaside summer fare.

Map: OS 1:50,000 Exeter and Sidmouth; Landranger no. 192.

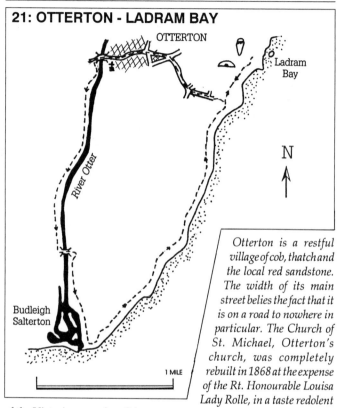

21: OTTERTON - LADRAM BAY

OTTERTON

Ladram
Bay

River Otter

N

Budleigh
Salterton

1 MILE

Otterton is a restful village of cob, thatch and the local red sandstone. The width of its main street belies the fact that it is on a road to nowhere in particular. The Church of St. Michael, Otterton's church, was completely rebuilt in 1868 at the expense of the Rt. Honourable Louisa Lady Rolle, in a taste redolent

of the Victorian age of confidence.

At least the house martins are happy, having set up nest in the church porch: a little pile of droppings underneath warns worshippers of the dangers of an unwanted visitation from on high, courtesy of the fledglings.

Walk down the main street past Otterton Mill with its working watermill over the small stone road bridge and turn left onto the footpath. You are now set fair to follow the River Otter on your left as it takes its course, in no hurry to reach the sea.

The Otter's flood plain is wide, bounded by low red sandstone cliffs on

Sea-stacks at Ladram Bay

the left bank. On a hot humid day I walked alongside its lazy waters, two swans sweated overhead, honking gently to the beat of their wings. Meanwhile a buzzard struggled to catch a thermal in the heavy air.

At the road bridge cross left and follow the footpath signs right that point to Ladram Bay, 3 miles distant. The path climbs alongside a strip of Scots pine.

Dissolving into its estuary below, the Otter disappears into the sea or low tide mud flats. Secreted under the pines is a bird watchers' hide, a boon for any ornithologist as it commands an unimpeded view of the estuary. As the pines thin, discreet and understated Budleigh Salterton comes into view. Where the Otter meets the sea it creeps rather apologetically round the shingle spit that has almost closed its mouth.

Turn your back upon this scene and follow the broad track, part of the South West Coastal Footpath uphill. Now the sea and its cliffs will remain on your right at all times until Ladram Bay. Gradually views of field-quilted East Devon open out.

Laid down many millions of years ago under desert conditions the local rock is known as the New Red Sandstone series. From its exposed cliff faces

95

the eddying effects of sea, salt, and wind have sculpted hollows and ledges upon which juvenile gulls are reared. At Ladram Bay the sea has broken into the land leaving behind a most picturesque collection of red rock seastacks with a sheltered cove and a sliver of shingle beach running for a quarter of a mile. By way of contrast the white chalk cliffs of Beer Head emerge out of the haze to the east.

The path has all this time been tending gently uphill but once through the shell of a derelict building starts to wander down to Ladram Bay, with its rather less picturesque mobile homes and ice cream kiosks.

Arriving on a beach in heavy boots and full walking regalia is a little incongruous, especially when the sun is out and one is faced with the scantily clad catching some rays. But frankly on a summer's day, I think nothing beats breaking for a swim. Remember though, even if the water is an inviting aquamarine, the temperature probably won't be. At Ladram the beach shelves so steeply that after just a few steps it is too late for the timorous and goose-pimpled, so there's nothing for it but to swim.

Upon recovery it is time for the short return leg. Fortunately this does not mean High Peak, which at over 450 feet affords stunning views across Sidmouth and East Devon, but not without the expenditure of a great deal of energy.

In fact it is the type of hill that sorts the men and women from the boys and girls. So men, women and imminent hernias straight on - the rest follow me.

All that remains is to retrace your steps up the hill you came down to reach Ladram Bay. At the top just before the hedge, turn right along a footpath signposted to Otterton three-quarters of a mile distant. Simply follow this track which part way along becomes metalled. At the end of it you will come to a T-junction. Turn right and at its end you will emerge at the eastern end of Otterton. Keep left for the main street.

Torcross and Slapton Ley (Walk 13) *(author)*
Start Point from Prawle Point (Walk 14) *(author)*

---

22. EAST DEVON:
Across Devon's chalk downland - Branscombe to Beer, a figure of eight round - 7 miles

---

Directions

Start:	Branscombe between Sidmouth and Seaton.
Outline and walk length:	A relatively easy 7 miles of cliff and country chalk downland which can be radically shortened by walking only one of the two loops. Allow three hours - longer if you pause to watch the fishing boats landing the daily catch in Beer.
Getting there:	From the A3052 follow the signs to Branscombe.
Parking:	Fee paying village/parish hall car park immediately left after the working forge and opposite the tea room and bakery.
Refreshments:	Branscombe has two pubs, the Mason's Arms and Fountain Head - the latter actually in Street, National Trust tea rooms and post office. Alternatively, Beer is well endowed with a number of pubs, cafes and restaurants.
Map:	OS 1:50,000 Exeter and Sidmouth; Landranger no. 192.

Rippling above and below the surface of southern England chalk makes its most westerly appearance at Branscombe, bringing with it a typical downland landscape. At Beer Head the cliffs are completely of chalk though the Keuper marl underneath makes it unstable. In March 1790 ten acres of Hooken Cliff slipped seaward dropping 200-260 feet and moving the shore out 200 yards.

Branscombe straggles down a long, sinuous wooded valley, almost to the sea at Branscombe Mouth. The village boasts a gorgeous church dedicated to an obscure 7th century Welsh saint, St. Winifred. Evidence of the religious schism at the root of the English Civil War is recorded on a plaque inside, listing previous vicars but noting that those between 1641 and 1660 were not legally appointed. There is much Norman stone work, some even pre-dates the Conquest, and with its rare box pews the church is particularly atmospheric. At Branscombe's western end is the tight thatched, cob hamlet of Street - sweet freshwater springs bubbling from the hillside.

A winter's evening in the Teign Gorge. (Walk 30)

The area was long associated with smugglers, Beer being a focal point. Nowadays small inshore trawlers set out from Beer's sheltered cove. After the catch is landed they are hauled up the shingle beach on thick steel ropes.

In the past fisher families would sit on their doorsteps lining the main street, gutting the day's catch and tossing the remains into the centre of the road where the now culverted stream used to spill across cobbles. The stench in high summer must have been incredible.

To start the walk, ignore the temptations of the National Trust tea rooms and leave the village hall car park, where there are toilets. Turn left onto the main road into the village and, just before the row of houses on the right, turn right where signposted to Branscombe Mouth. This well worn path follows a stream which it crosses halfway down, coming out behind a cafe facing the beach.

Turn to your left across the stream's mouth where there is an information board and signposted footpath to Beer. Follow the path uphill before taking the lower official coastal footpath on the right through a gaggle of mobile homes that perch on an old land-slip, once used by the villagers for their early potatoes. Follow the path through thick but low vegetation past Hooken land-slip.

Ahead is about 2 miles of shattered chalk and, once away from the mobile homes, you can look to your left at the fissures and cracks that will surely bring tons of rubble down in some future storm. Also to your left a dark adit, halfway up the cliff, drains the caverns of Beer Quarry which in

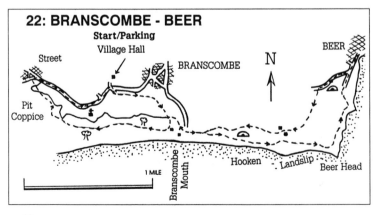

its time provided stone for Exeter and Winchester Cathedrals, as well as the majority of East Devon's churches.

The path continues to wind through the thick but low vegetation, climbing slowly between the pinnacles of Hooken land-slip. The 1790 collapse had the effect of pushing up a great ridge of sea bed. The morning following the slip fishermen returned to find that the crab pots laid the previous evening 8-10 feet under water were now high and dry 15 feet in the air.

Shortly after the pinnacles on your right, the path climbs briskly and affords open views back to Branscombe Mouth. If you are lucky you may spot the sabre-winged peregrine falcon, a magnificent sight, and of one Britain's rarest hawks.

Soon you will reach the cliff top. The path now curves across grassy downland towards Beer which, thirst-generated, you should reach poste haste, via a field of mobile homes and steeply descending road.

I first visited Beer a few years ago and after the tourism of Exmouth, gentility of Sidmouth and wonderful dilapidation of Seaton, the last thing I expected to find was a small, still working fishing village. While the visitor is an important commodity to Beer traders, it is a joy to be able to watch catches being landed. And if you are so inclined, a variety of caught-today fish and shellfish can be bought down at the beachhead.

Like so many places that are now polite and law abiding, Beer takes pride in some of the more dubious activities of its past citizens, thankful that they add "character" today without the threat of violence or the law's long arm. Here it is the celebrated smuggling exploits of 18th Century local ne'er-do-well Jack Rattenbury. Rather grimly, the village's history includes the customs officer who "fell" off his horse and "drowned" in broad daylight in the stream dribbling down the main street and another officer laid to rest in Branscombe churchyard, having taken a fatal cliff tumble while attempting to extinguish a smuggler's signal fire.

Having lingered amid the flint napped cottages and stately Victorian holiday homes of Beer, it is time for the return leg. Retrace your steps up the road to the fields of mobile homes, but instead of turning left along the metalled footpath by which you entered Beer, carry on up the hill past the holiday camp.

Eventually, the road runs into track near the hill's top and you should take the left fork across grassland where the rare bee orchid

Fishing boats pulled up on the beach at Beer

can be found, back to Branscombe. As you do so you will pass a low stone whitewashed building and a curious grey tower. Upon cresting the ridge there are glorious views over Branscombe, to Sidmouth and beyond.

Once you have descended the steep section of path back to Branscombe Mouth, you can either complete the second loop or, if already over-exerted, return via path or road to Branscombe.

If having been reinvigorated by the sound of clattering pebbles tugged by the sea at Branscombe Mouth and the short stretch over the cliffs to Branscombe church is tempting, then return to the track behind the cafe, leaving it left to ascend the hillside by the signposted footpath.

Two Second World War bunkers or pill-boxes guard the beach and it is worth popping inside the one nearest the path above the cafe. Next to one of the slits is a faint pencil diagram of semi-circles, with range markers to the opposite hillside and beach.

Leaving this coastal defence, return to the path and at its top turn round to survey the scene, with Hooken land-slip and Beer Head directly due east. The path soon levels out and runs under mature woodland. Glimpses of cottages and the church can be had through the strong limbed branches of beech trees.

To reach Street follow the main path onto open ground taking the right fork where it branches and following signs as directed through Pit Coppice over a number of stiles to the thatched hamlet. From Street follow the road back to Branscombe.

---

23. EAST DEVON:
A Devon jungle - the Undercliff from Seaton to Lyme Regis.
Linear route - 7 miles

Directions

Start:	Seaton, East Devon.
Outline and walk length:	Along the Undercliff - magnificent coastal woodland - one of the finest walks in Devon, possibly the country. Fairly arduous going for 7 miles over the complex chasms of this densely wooded land-slump. Allow at least four hours, longer for a good wander round Lyme Regis. Return by bus (see below) or if fit along the cliff path in which case double all times.
Parking:	Fee car park in Seaton behind the sea front.
Refreshments:	None on walk but a full range of pubs and shops can be found in Seaton and Lyme Regis.
Map:	Landranger no. 193; OS Taunton and Lyme Regis 1:50,000.
The Return:	From the bottom of Broad Street in Lyme Regis, the area called The Square: take the No. 899 Axe Valley Coaches service to Seaton and Sidmouth. There are regular departures but check running times through the Devon General Rural Bus Service information line in Exeter.

Sulphur, flame, lightning and the roaring sound of the land cracking asunder filled the air, reported observers, as the huge land-slip of Christmas night 1839 created the Undercliff. That night it is estimated 8 million tons of rock slid. Twenty acres moved and 15 remained intact suddenly much closer to the sea. So apocalyptic seemed the event that the Book of Revelations was invoked.

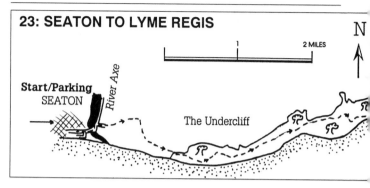

23: SEATON TO LYME REGIS

N

2 MILES

Start/Parking
SEATON

River Axe

The Undercliff

The slip was caused by a water saturated lower layer of yellowish greensands called Foxmould giving way and taking with it other layers of greensand and chalk above. A walk along the Undercliff today is utterly magical. The stone homes of labourers who farmed the slip for some years afterwards are romantic ruins. Now ungrazed, the undergrowth is lush and verdant. The footpath switches back and forth between the pinnacles and chasms left by the slip, and, forming an impenetrable wall inland, the geologically recent cliffs of 1839 still look fresh.

Leaving Seaton walking east along the B3172 you will pass the attractive harbour of Axmouth and the handful of yachts sheltering behind the high shingle beach that has almost closed the river's mouth.

The road bends to the left over the river, just after which and signposted to Lyme Regis you should turn right up a steep fitness-testing hill, the track being asphalted up to Axmouth Golf Club. Carry straight on past the club house, going right and then left where signposted across the golf course - keeping your fingers crossed that the players have decent handicaps and their drives are not too errant.

Once across the course, pass on to the track between two hedges, which you should leave turning right where signposted to Lyme Regis some 7 miles away. The path falls gently and upon entering a field follows the left-hand edge. The route, waymarked with yellow arrows, bears left again, bringing you out upon the cliff's edge above thick woodland.

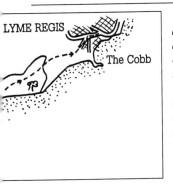

LYME REGIS

The Cobb

Before continuing, survey the views west around the sweep of Torbay and east as far as Portland, and then descend into the other world that is the Undercliff, a place of surprises.

Successive slumps and slides have ensured that the Undercliff is a complex of fissures, chasms, cliffs and "islands" of rock, "Goat Island" and "The Chasm" formed in 1839 the most notable. The area was designated a National Nature Reserve in 1955.

The path, always easy to follow, falls into the undergrowth and winds up and down steadily eastward. At times the sea is in sight and sound - in other places the path climbs "islands" of rock with lush chasms either side.

Slender ash trees burdened with ivy and creepers sway and creak, in a wind whose breath fails to stir the thicket of the woodland floor. The intensely luxuriant growth of plantlife probably gives a good idea of how all the southern lowlands once looked, before early people began their slash and burn clearances, which have culminated today in the intensive monoculture of modern farming.

At the halfway stage through the Undercliff there is a second Nature Reserve noticeboard near a single red-brick cottage chimney, rather romantic in its setting.

The path follows a track a short distance before turning right uphill, and, once again clearly signposted, passing a thick stand of horse-tail ferns.

From the path, dappled with sunlight and then sunk in gloom, look out on the right for the shell of another cottage. If the woods seem familiar it is worth remembering that the film of John Fowle's novel The French Lieutenant's Woman *was filmed here. In Lyme Regis many of the "Victorianized" shop fronts installed for the filming have been retained.*

The path passes a small creamy coloured corrugated building humming with the production of electricity before following its service road uphill, from which you should turn off right back onto the path once again signposted.

Here there are breaks in the trees, and the cliffs at Charmouth, Chesil

103

Beach and Portland are all to be seen, no longer just outlines on the horizon.

Soon you will leave the Undercliff proper: as you do so the path divides, and while either may be chosen take the lower one and then go right through the gate opposite the bungalow selling honey, and over the last stretch of open ground, at last released from the wood's shadow.

After descending the path goes through two gates, turning right at the second and running between houses a short way to a car park, at the top of Lyme Regis.

In the town a stroll out along the famous Cobb is a must. As is visiting the antiquarian shops selling all manner of fossilized animals and plants - even, rather bizarrely, the fossilized droppings of turtles, as well as smaller examples of the Ichthyosaur, a fish-like reptile found nearby by Mary Anning in 1809.

To return to Seaton the choice is simple enough: back the same way on foot, which I'm sure is thoroughly fulfilling.

Or spend 15 minutes on a number 899 bus to Seaton, which demonstrates one of the advantages of burning fossil fuels...

---

24. EAST DEVON:
A tramp up the Otter to its healthland heights - Otterton to Mutters Moor and return via Peak Hill - 9 miles

---

Directions

Start:	Otterton, between Budleigh Salterton and Sidmouth.
Outline and walk length:	Upstream along the River Otter, climbing onto the East Devon heaths, returning via the red cliffs of High Peak and Ladram Bay. Mostly level but with one stiff climb from Newton Poppleford to Mutters Moor, 9 miles in all. Allow four hours.
Parking:	Main street in Otterton.
Refreshments:	Plenty on route. Otterton has a pub and general store as well as Otterton Mill and restaurant. Colaton Raleigh has a pub and Newton Poppleford pubs and shops. At Ladram Bay there is a bar and assorted purveyors of ice cream.
Map:	OS 1:50,000 Exeter and Sidmouth; Landranger no. 192.

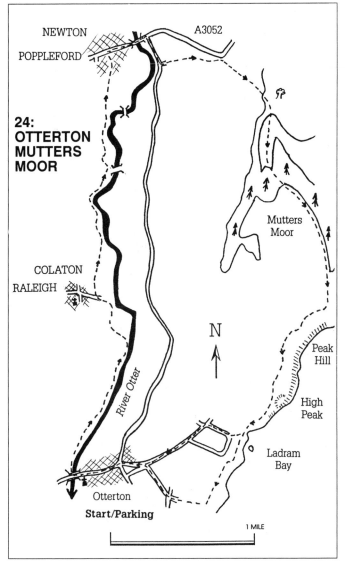

NEWTON

POPPLEFORD

A3052

**24:
OTTERTON
MUTTERS
MOOR**

Mutters
Moor

COLATON

RALEIGH

River Otter

N

Peak
Hill

High
Peak

Ladram
Bay

Otterton

Start/Parking

1 MILE

Leave the lovely village of Otterton by walking down the main street to the River Otter, crossing over the bridge and turn right to walk upstream so that the river is on your right.

Idling its last miles to the sea down this most gentle of valleys the Otter tumbles over a low weir, the sound of falling water a faint echo of far greater waterfalls the world over. Overhung with oak and beech its eastern bank is a wall of red sandstone.

At one point the river is spanned by a graceful wooden bridge sweeping to the opposite side - ending 20 feet higher than the bank from which it started. Where the Otter struggles to carry its sediment load, small islands form, braiding its flow. In other places great stands of bright pink flowered Himalayan Balsam choke its passage.

Eventually you will have to leave the river's bank, and where signposted follow the footpath to Colaton Raleigh. As you pass the village's first houses the footpath you need to follow to Newton Poppleford is on the right.

Yet it is worth walking a little further into Colaton Raleigh, an attractive village of thatch and cob. The Church of St. John the Baptist was largely rebuilt by the Victorians in 1875. It retains its Norman font and striking 19th century wall carvings. Grapes, leaves, arches, studs and flowers have been carved into the sandstone then picked out and painted in mauve, blue and green.

Having paused, retrace your steps to the Newton Poppleford footpath, which will now be on your left as you come from the church. The path climbs gently and where there are breaks in the hedge glimpses can be had across the Otter's floodplain to High Peak. The path levels out and bears right into a field. The hedge is now on your left, but carry on straight ahead, over a stile - signposted to Newton Poppleford a mile distant. The path passes through a gate, descends and then you turn right, over another stile and into a meadow which you should cross, bearing left to the stile ahead - in the right-hand corner of the meadow. At the stile go left up a lane and then right as signposted.

The River Otter is still on your right, and the path, worn by the tread of sheep, rises under trees. Go left up a flight of steps and then right. You will now find yourself above the river upon a line of cliffs and trees. The flood plain below is studded with the disused railway bridges of a long redundant line.

On your left, or at least when I passed by, is a large field of peas, bent over, blackbirds skittering between the stalks. Keep straight ahead and the path crosses a small wooden footbridge just to the right, before becoming metalled and passing at the bottom of a number of gardens into Newton Poppleford.

Turn right at its end onto the A3052 crossing the Otter via the road bridge with care as there is no pavement. At the first lane after the bridge turn right. The River Otter should now be on your right as you face downstream, though its company you will soon be leaving.

Immediately before Northmostown Farm go left up a rough metalled track. The climb is steep, but it is the walk's only bout of toil. At the track's end bear right, signposted to Bulverton Hill via Back Lane.

As you climb, good views down the Otter open out. At the level summit go right and then almost immediately left, signposted to Peak Hill, one and a quarter miles distant along a public bridleway. As you walk, Bulverton Hill merges into Mutters Moor - an outstanding example of lowland heath, now nationally very rare.

Where open the moor is covered in cross-leaved heather, gorse and broom; in other places Scots pine and shimmering silver birch dominate. The thin sandy soil is a favourite of adders, and at dusk the sky is patrolled by the nightjar.

The path goes left a little, then right, where it merges with others but remains wide, flinty and broadly straight on. Eventually you will come to a small car park. Cross the road and walk to the end of what is Peak Hill where it collapses into the sea.

The views are glorious along the coast east. Looking west the foreground is dominated by the seaward flank of High Peak, eroded into sharp bare ribs of brilliant red sandstone - a bedrock skeleton stripped of earth, woodland hanging precipitously above the plunging gullies.

From here it is but a short return to Otterton. Turn right, or to the west and High Peak. Upon entering the woods at the foot of High Peak there is a bench with wonderful views east to Sidmouth and beyond.

You can return to Otterton from here either by bearing right down a track signposted to the village or by skirting the summit of High Peak and dropping down to Ladram Bay and a deserved ice cream halt. Return to Otterton via the camp road - or alternatively the footpath just south of Ladram Bay which was described in Walk no. 21.

---

25. EAST DEVON:
Over the Blackdown Hills - Hemyock, Wellington Memorial and Culmstock Beacon round - 9 miles

---

Directions

Start: Hemyock in the Culm Valley, south of the Blackdown Hills on the edge of the Devon/Somerset border, north-east of Tiverton.

Outline and
walk length: A stroll through the sumptuous Blackdown Hills, climbing to the Wellington Memorial just inside Somerset - excellent views north over Taunton and to Exmoor. Return via Culmstock Beacon, one of the finest viewpoints in all Devon. A relatively easy walk of 9 miles with only one long uphill pull onto the top of the Blackdowns. Allow four to five hours.

Getting there: From the M5 turn off at Junction 27 on to the A38 Wellington road, from which you should eventually turn right onto the B3391 signposted to Culmstock and Hemyock.

Parking: Free public car park in the centre of Hemyock on the right, past the Victorian 'pump'.

Refreshments: In Hemyock there are two village stores, a petrol station, and one pub, the Catherine Wheel. No refreshments on the walk unless you divert to Culmstock.

Map: OS 1:50,000 Taunton and Lyme Regis;
                Landranger no. 103.

Hemyock sits in the graceful valley of the River Culm, an ancient settlement of Celtic or Saxon origin called Hamihoc in the Domesday book of 1086.

At its centre, painted thickly in bright yellow and green paint, is the Hemyock pump. Erected in 1902 it is a catch-all memorial managing to commemorate peace in South Africa at the end of the Boer War, the reign of Queen Victoria, and the coronation of Edward VII all at once.

The Knights of St. Catherine - founded in 1063 to protect pilgrims on their journeys to the Holy Land - gave their name to the Catherine Wheel pub. Their badge was a white surplice bearing a wheel armed with spikes and traversed by a sword stained with blood. While no doubt reassuring travellers of the Crusades, today we make do with the rather more prosaic and less bloody AA badge.

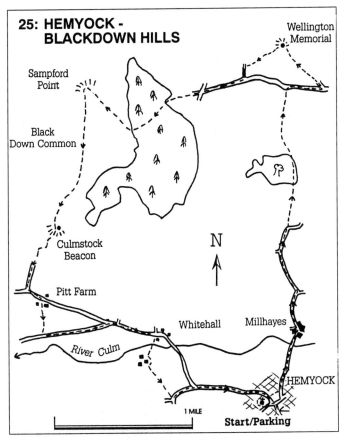

Leaving the public car park, walk back to the centre of the village past the pump and Catherine Wheel pub. After the Church of St. Mary on your right, turn right onto the footpath next to the village stream, which drains the disconcertingly named little valley of Lickham Bottom. On your left are the remains of Hemyock Castle. More a fortified house built in the late 13th or early 14th century and open in the afternoons between Easter and September.

At the end of the short path cross over the road and walk down the signposted footpath immediately before the petrol station. At its end, turn left and walk down the gentle hill to Millhayes, past the old milk depot (now St. Ivel) once served by the Culm Valley railway, which opened in 1876 and was shut tantalisingly close to its 100th birthday in 1975.

Now begins the long but fairly modest climb to the Wellington Memorial, which for the purpose of this walk has been annexed from Somerset to qualify as a Devon walk.

Walk directly uphill. Near its summit, where the road turns sharp right, you turn sharp left. The road that you are now on is fairly level, running past the occasional house and giving glimpses of Culmstock Beacon opposite. Shortly it bears right, uphill. Near the top as the road continues to bear right, carry straight on to a signposted footpath. At the time of writing there was no gate here but that may change.

The path is a broad grassy track running along the edge of a ridge under beech, oak and holly wood with dock leaves thoughtfully provided by nature to soothe sore shins stung by nettles. Suddenly, having picked your way through the leaf litter, the pale-creamy point of the Wellington obelisk thrusts into sight.

At the path's end, cross a stile and turn right along the road and after 400 yards or so, left through the National Trust car park to the base of the Wellington Memorial.

We remember the Duke of Wellington as the vanquisher of Napoleon, and 19th century English hero number one, conveniently forgetting that he was in fact from an old Irish family whose links with the town of Wellington ended in the 14th century. His dukedom was conferred by a grateful nation in thanks for his military achievements but despite purchasing an estate in the vicinity of Wellington he only visited the town once. Local aristocracy hatched the memorial idea but while their grandiose scheme was started in 1817 their funds were somewhat less grandiose and the project was not completed until 1894.

Attempts were made to mount various cannons at the 175 foot high memorial's base, but the wrong ones were delivered to Exeter, some of which were later buried to become the bollards on Exeter Quay.

It is interesting to note that graffiti pre-dates even the birth of those who bemoan the "decline in standards" - the base is well and truly carved by 19th century vandals.

The views north over Somerset are excellent though. Dunkery Beacon, its highest point, can clearly be seen, as well as, on what would have to be a very clear day, the Black Mountains of South Wales - 70 miles distant. The town of Wellington is immediately below the summit.

On leaving the memorial you have a choice of two paths to the right behind the small car park. The official path marked on the map leads over a gate and through a field back to the road, but better is the TBDC (Taunton Borough District Council) signposted path down through the woods, the way showered with pine cone cores by a voracious grey squirrel. The path turns right where a field, or rather a hopeless patch of bare soil, is home to a number of sows.

Just past the field, turn left onto a bridleway which leads back to the road. Unfortunately, this track is used by large herds of "migrating" cattle; as a result it is the sort of quagmire that you really will not want to step into, so delicate manoeuvring round its edge is required. At its end turn right onto the road and simply walk in a straight line for about half a mile, turning neither left nor right until it runs out into a dirt track which skirts the edge of a small plantation of coniferous woodland.

The track now climbs gently and curves to the left. At its top take the track that runs to the right of the radio mast, 100 yards on from which will bring you to the thin, flinty-soiled plateau of Black Down Common, clad in purple heather and golden gorse.

If you now walk north-east along an easily defined track, you will come to Sampford Point. While having less extensive views than the Wellington Memorial, they are uninterrupted by trees.

Retrace your steps, cross and follow a wide grassy track which was a failed attempt at a racecourse. This runs along the top of the Common between high stands of bracken upon which marble white butterflies dance. Follow the track to its end but continue along the

Culmstock Beacon - one of the finest viewpoints in all Devon

top of the plateau following either the left or right edge paths that wind round to Culmstock Beacon.

A circular, flint-walled and roofed "hut" marks Culmstock Beacon, which is one of the best viewpoints in all Devon. From its summit the Blackdown Hills unfold south and east; the hills of Mid Devon to the west; and directly beyond the Culm Valley towards Exeter, the Haldon Hills forming the wall at the city's back. The sandy soils of the ridge heat up rapidly in summer, energising insect life and butterflies in frantic communion.

Leave the Beacon by the steep path directly below its peak. At its foot there is a choice of returns to Hemyock. If the map is to be believed, it is possible to follow a footpath that starts the Beacon side of the hedge and runs to Pithayne Farm. Personally I have found this overgrown. Instead, about 10 yards to the right, is a small road which should be followed to the hill's foot.

If you require a completely trouble-free return, then turn right and make your way to Culmstock and thence to Hemyock. Alternatively, turn left towards Pitt Farm.

Just after the bungalow, and immediately before the first farm building, turn right down what is, although not signposted, an official footpath. To follow this you will have to pass through three field gates. As a reward you may see a little owl, our smallest resident owl, perched upon a fence.

Once over the last gate, simply turn left onto the road. This leads to the hamlet of Whitehall, before which, on the right, a footpath crosses the River Culm by a series of small footbridges and leads to the main Culmstock to Hemyock road, a left turn taking you back to the start.

---

26. MID DEVON:
Across the fields and daffodil woods of Tedburn St. Mary -
4 miles

Direction

Start:	Tedburn St. Mary, north of the A30 Exeter to Okehampton road.
Outline and walk length:	A gentle potter round the hills of Mid Devon returning along the Lilly Brook. About 4 miles of track and field walking. Allow two hours.
Getting there:	From Exeter or Okehampton take the A30, turning off and following the signs to Tedburn St. Mary.
By Bus:	Devon General service no. 51 and South Western service no. 359.
Parking:	In village.
Refreshment:	In Tedburn two pubs, the Village Inn and the Kings Arms, plus general stores.
Map:	OS 1:25,000 Exeter, Pathfinder 1314 or OS 1:50,000 Okehampton and North Dartmoor, Landranger no. 191.

Many footpaths crossing the mild-mannered hills and steep combes of Mid Devon go unwalked due to the understandable rush to tramp moor and coast. This is a great pity. Hidden in the quiet woods going about their business are deer, badgers, foxes and so many other animals. The softly treading walker has a far greater chance of coming upon these creatures in the rarely visited countryside than on either cliff or tor.

113

26: TEDBURN ST MARY

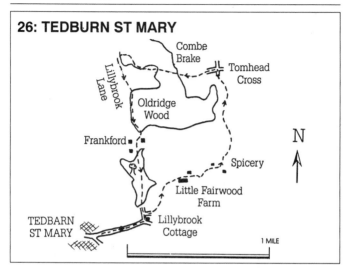

Leave Tedburn St. Mary by the road signposted to Whitestone. The road runs downhill. On your right you will pass Lower Uppacott Farm and a sign enticing you to purchase a firkin or two of the local cider. At the bottom of the hill cross a stone bridge and turn left down the footpath so that Lillybrook Cottage is on your right. Turn right almost immediately past the cottage up a metalled lane and footpath leading to Little Fairwood Farm.

Come autumn chill the hedgerow greens are replaced through icy stealth with russets and browns. Fallen leaves chatter together stirred by the wind. Unpicked blackberries silently souring lie thick upon the brambles.

The path-cum-lane passes Little Fairwood Farm, going through a couple of gates in the process, before passing in front of a row of pretty and very secluded cottages. Here the asphalt runs out onto a track which bears right and joins another onto which you should turn left. This track leads to a small farm called Spicery on the OS map and you go straight on through two metal gates and cattle yard. The path falls then bears left between high hedges, the going muddy in places. At the track's end, pass through a gate into an open field. On your right is a thick copse, the silence broken by a wood pigeon's clattering flight as it breaks cover.

Follow the hedge on your left downhill, ignoring the first gate on the left until you reach another, which once through puts you at a brook's edge. Cross and follow the path uphill; as you do so fine views over the hills and fields behind unfold. At the path's top there is a gate leading you out to a junction, Tomhead Cross, where you should turn left. Now the track-cum-bridleway runs between two hedges.

At its end there is a gate leading into an open wood, Combe Brake. Walk roughly straight ahead, so that the rusting farm machinery, waiting for the nostalgic "bygone collectors" to appear and save it before it completely disappears, is on your right. On reaching a gate pass through keeping to the hedge right, as you walk downhill. At another gate, either pass through and follow the sunken, and in places rather overgrown, green lane downhill; alternatively go a little past the gate and then right and follow a path that runs alongside the sunken lane. It is difficult to tell from the OS map which is the correct route though there is little to choose between the two. At the bottom go left.

This is Lillybrook Lane and after rain so submerged can it become that a swimming certificate should be clutched as a lucky charm against falling in. Progress is possible along the track's edge, though you may attract the attention of a herd of cows in the adjacent field, enjoying the entertainment and willing, in a bovine sort of way, your watery demise. Jokes and precariousness aside, once over this obstacle it's plain sailing - if it hasn't been plain wading already.

The track opens out but carry straight on. Where it starts to curve to the left and climb, leave it bearing right down a distinct if not actually signposted footpath.

The path runs through Oldridge Wood, or the Daffodil Woods as they are known to locals, with Lilly Brook on your right. Sun dappled on a still day, birdsong, butterflies and "flying-pencil" dragonflies entertain. Scanning the narrow path at your feet you should see the hoof prints of deer.

Where the path enters a clearing go right over a small wooden footbridge which crosses the brook. Follow the path round and where it comes out in front of a house go right. You will shortly arrive at a track junction. To your right are the few houses that make up Frankford. But you carry straight on, following the track alongside the Lilly Brook until you pass Lillybrook Cottage at the walk's beginning.

---

27. MID DEVON:
To the heart of the River Teign's old mines - Bridford and Christow round - 5 miles

---

Directions

Start: Bridford on the western valley side of the River Teign just inside the Dartmoor National Park.

Outline and
walk length: An easy footpath and lane stroll across the flanks of the River Teign Valley, taking in the villages of Bridford and Christow as well as the remnants of a number of old mines. The main route is 5 miles long, 3.5 miles only if you miss one of the mines. Allow two to four hours.

Getting there: From the A38 in the south or B3212 in the north turn onto the B3193 then signs to Bridford.

Parking: In Bridford where parking is limited so please park with consideration.

Refreshments: Watering holes at the Bridford Inn, Bridford, and the Artichoke Inn, Christow, and general stores in both villages.

Map: The OS 1:50,000 Okehampton and North Dartmoor sheet no. 191 will just about do but the OS 1:25,000 Pathfinder Dunsford and Kenton map provides far greater detail.

The River Teign rushes off Dartmoor, squeezes through its gorge and then pauses for breath, meandering through the meadows of its middle reach.

East rise the Haldon Hills and west the National Park's edge. Crouching in the folds of the valley's flanks a number of unspoilt and largely unvisited villages retain a remoteness that belies their proximity to the urban centres of Exeter and Newton Abbot.

The valley experienced an industrial boom in the 19th century when dozens of small mines sprang up to exploit the reserves of silver, lead, copper, manganese, iron and barytes ores. From 1830 to the closure of the last mine in 1970 the gloom of winter nights was daily pierced by the miner's lamp as he tramped home from the minehead. Village populations soared during this period. By 1861 Christow had a population of 941 and Hennock 1004. By the end of the 19th century many of the smaller mines had already closed and their remains were demolished or left to crumble away.

Nevertheless surface buildings and adits can still be found and this walk allows a ramble through unspoilt, if not untouched, countryside past various mine remains.

Before leaving Bridford visit the church of St. Thomas a Beckett, up a flight of steps to the right of the curious "Angler's Cottage", an almost triangular building. The church contains an exquisitely carved rood screen with some figures still carrying their original colouring, though the church guide notes that their faces were mutilated by Puritan soldiers.

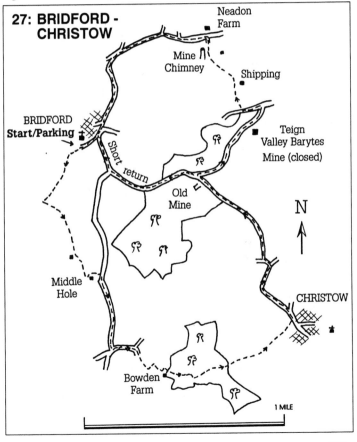

27: BRIDFORD - CHRISTOW

Neadon Farm

Mine Chimney

Shipping

BRIDFORD
Start/Parking

Short return

Teign Valley Barytes Mine (closed)

Old Mine

N

Middle Hole

CHRISTOW

Bowden Farm

1 MILE

The walk itself passes in front of the Bridford Inn, downhill past the old rectory where the road runs out and becomes a bridleway. Follow this hazelnut scattered track and stay on it as it bears left signposted as a bridleway to Middle Hole. Here once again it becomes metalled as it climbs gently, giving views back to Bridford.

Walk past the front of Lower Hole Farm and up to the end of the track, where you should turn left through a gate and past Middle Hole Farm with its well dressed scarecrows. Close the gate and turn right onto the road which, after a gentle climb, provides fine views back to the Haldon Hills and the white tower of Lawrence Castle. At the end of the road turn left and then after 100 yards, right through the gated field signposted as a bridleway. Stick to the "letter" of the path by walking the equivalent of two sides of a rectangle, even though the same feat could be accomplished by walking diagonally across the field to its corner.

Having regained the farm track, walk to the left of Bowden Farm, noting the granite corn grind stones, and continue along the bridleway, past the front of the main farmhouse. After a few hundred yards there is a stile and footpath left running alongside a steeply descending brook, the way marked periodically by yellow spots.

This is a pretty spot with mossy rocks and a brook, plus fallen oaks still in leaf despite their trunks almost completely uprooted.

The path descends over a number of stiles, an open field and fords the stream right before running along the right bank into Christow.

To your right is the Artichoke Inn, or descending the hill, refreshment of a more spiritual nature at the Church of St. James. But to return to Bridford turn left at the lane and left again uphill past the local primary school via Dry Lane.

Just over the crest turn left and follow the signposted lane back to Bridford.

Walking along the lane one day I came across a most confident fox in the neighbouring field, who after sizing me up, took his ease amongst the sheep for 10 minutes before disappearing into the undergrowth.

On the left, set just back from and above the level of the road on private land, are the remains of a small lead-silver mine, shrouded in thick brambles. A more readily visible redundant mine can be reached by taking

The stunted chimney and ore dressing room of the lead-silver mine near Bridford

the walk extension.

You will come to a junction - a left turn uphill along a wooded lane will bring you to Bridford, but to visit the redundant mine turn sharp right and almost back upon yourself.

You will now be heading directly away from Bridford but as you do so look to your right and down to see the remains of the Teign Valley Barytes Mine, closed in 1958. In its time this was a highly productive mine employing 100 raising barytes - barium sulphate, used in the manufacture of paint, hydrogen peroxide and the drilling operations of oil wells. The settling lagoons and some of the outbuildings are still visible on the barren 9 acre site surface, a raw open wound in the otherwise green skin of the Teign Valley.

At the next junction, turn sharp left uphill and then very shortly right along a track and official footpath. As the track turns to Shipping carry straight on through a gate and into a field that may or may not be full of inquisitive cattle. Walk straight across to the farthest corner of the field directly opposite, where there is an iron barred stile. Across the stile follow the path past a small pond on the right up to another redundant lead-silver mine.

A stunted granite chimney, embraced by ivy, is today dwarfed by the ash and oak which have sprung up since the mine entered its years of silence. Nearby is the ruin of a once solid granite building, possibly the mine manager's house or more likely an ore dressing room, where the metal bearing lode was separated from waste rock.

From the mine walk straight uphill on a mostly metalled track leading to another lane opposite which is Neadon Farm. Turn left uphill and follow the lane between high hedges as it curves back to Bridford.

---

28. MID DEVON:
In search of Tarka - The River Taw from Nymet Rowland and Coldridge - 6 miles

Directions

Start: Nymet Rowland, near Lapford.

Outline and walk length:	Across the backwater hills of Mid Devon, along the River Taw and Tarka Trail. Some 6 miles, allow three to four hours.
Getting there:	From the A377 north of Crediton follow the signs from near Lapford to Nymet Rowland.
Parking:	On road signposted to Coldridge near Nymet Rowland church.
Refreshments:	Post office and general store in Coldridge.
Map:	OS 1:50,000 Okehampton and North Dartmoor; Landranger no. 191.

Bypassed in the rush to shore and moor Mid Devon hides some of the deepest silences and little walked paths of all Devon. Of course little walked on the ground often means overgrown and poorly signposted, but this route, taking in a chunk of the Tarka Trail along the River Taw, repays the walker's effort in map juggling - not with the spectacular or dramatically bleak but in its unvisited, overlooked pastoral gentleness.

Baying otter hounds no longer crash through the Taw's shallow waters but it remains an incredibly lucky walker who comes upon an otter while tramping along the ground which inspired Henry Williamson. Yet so little walked is Mid Devon that finding some of Britain's larger native mammals in broad daylight is a real prospect. While walking this route one cloudy August day I had the joy of watching a fox watch me as I lumbered by and later a badger shuffling through the woodland gloom a few feet across my path.

Undulating farmland rolls away from Nymet Rowland with the bluff shape of Cosdon Beacon, Dartmoor's fringe forming the southern backdrop. For me, still summer air punctuated by the buzzing drone of insects, the flick-flick-flick of a sprinkler watering the old rectory lawn and a distant chugging tractor mowing hay completes the scene.

With the church at your back walk down the lane signposted to Coldridge. Just past an oak tree are two gates on your right. Through the second is a signposted footpath which you should follow; the signpost may be concealed by the hedge.

Ahead is your first goal, the tower of St. Matthew's Church, Coldridge rising above a wood in the foreground.

Follow the hedge right, to a stile. Cross over and bear left over an area potentially marshy after heavy rain to a small gate and wooden footbridge over a stream. Walk uphill keeping the wood on your right.

Towards the hill's summit you will have to climb a wooden fence-cum-stile, the path marked with yellow arrows. After a short stretch under mixed woodland exit via a gate, keeping the line of trees on your right. The path, rather faint but still traceable, crosses a field of grass bearing left diagonally to a gate located near a white house on the extreme left of the church.

From the ridge, field and hedge lines amble east to Nymet Rowland and Lapford. Dartmoor broods heavily. Coldridge is a collection of lovely thatched cottages and a few modern homes. According to Devon historian Risdon, writing in his Survey of the County of Devon *completed some three hundred years ago, Coldridge's name is derived from the poor quality of its soil.*

The Church of St. Matthew is in W.C. Hoskins' words "graceful and well proportioned". Despite the modernising tendencies of the Victorians much of the original 15th and 16th century features were retained. The font is 13th century and thought to be Norman.

The church is gorgeous inside with bare wood waggon vaulting. Of particular note is the tracery of the rood screen and oak pulpit, both 15th

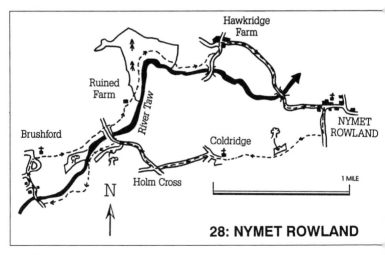

28: NYMET ROWLAND

century and unpainted. Look out for the medieval pews, their ends rather crudely carved and one sporting a curiously proportioned bearded face.

The parclose screen dividing the Evans chapel and its incumbent, a park-keeper of the Marquess of Dorset's deer park at Coldridge, from the chancel, is of a rare kind normally found in Brittany, with delicate un-English tracery. The glass above the table-tomb and effigy of Sir John Evans has been dated to 1480 and is believed to show Prince Edward, son of Edward IV.

Before leaving stand in the Barton Chapel with your back to the altar. If you examine the screen over the doorway you will find upside down the carved head of a lady - with her tongue rather grotesquely hanging out - the medieval carver taking revenge on a local scold?

Bell-ringing is big amongst Coldridge villagers if the number of certificates and prizes mounted upon the wall near the tower are anything to go by. The churchyard is dominated by some huge yew trees.

On leaving pass thatched cottages near the church and village green. Walk to the end of the green and go right. Follow the Eggesford road as signposted, then left signposted to Brushford past a row of thatched cottages.

Walk along the lane until you reach the junction at Holm Cross and turn right. Immediately after a wood on the left and before the lane greets a bridge over the River Taw turn left along a grassy track. Though not especially well signposted this track is part of the Tarka Trail. Keeping the wood on your left the path comes to a stile and gate adjacent to a small disused quarry.

Once over the stile follow the River Taw upstream walking along the edge of the field. Here the Taw bubbles darkly under its thick canopy of trees. Dragonflies manoeuvre their crayon thick bodies through a field of maize. Ignore the admittedly limited temptation to cross the Taw presented by a ford. Eventually you will come to a gated footbridge over a tributary stream. The farmhouse glimpsed across the fields and river is the immediate goal.

Leave the Taw and follow the hedge right, which eventually leaves the river and runs up to a gate with a yellow arrow waymarker.

Through the gate cross the field to the corner directly opposite about 75 yards away. Do not bear left to the low hill or clump of trees nearby. Though hidden when you set out, at the hedge you will see straight ahead a sunken track. Walk down it a few yards and turn right past a gatepost marked with a yellow arrow. Follow the track between high hedges until you come to the Taw which the walker is carried over by a footbridge.

The sense of wandering through a backwater untouched by the ripples of the wider world is overwhelming, if ultimately misguided, as any farmer who battles with summer droughts, set-aside and uncertain subsidy would swear.

Over the Taw you will come to a farm. Its neighbouring field is a graveyard of lorries and vans - where motors have crawled off to die as rusty as the dry stalked dock leaves shrouding their bodywork.

Keep the rather tumbledown farm on your left. Walk uphill along the track which becomes progressively more grassy underfoot. Through a gate carry straight on - on the map it looks like a right turn. The track becomes metalled and after houses left and right, turn right down a concreted driveway signposted "To the Church".

Brushford is scarcely a village, more an extended farmstead, and the Church of St. Mary more a chapel than church in size. It has a most curious slated semi-steeple tower, a replacement for the original spire destroyed in the 17th century. The church, dark, cool and silent inside, merely concentrates a sense of magical remoteness - as if by accident you have stumbled upon a lost world. It was over-restored by the Victorians in 1876-7 but the delicate tracery of the rood screen, similar to the parclose screen at Coldridge and almost unique but for a parallel at St. Fiacre-le-Faouet in Brittany, is worth stopping for. A key to get in can be had from the old rectory nextdoor.

Upon leaving the church turn left along a track and through a gate. Follow the hedge on your right along the ridge, enjoying some fine field and mixed-woodland views. Walk downhill and when confronted by a hedge directly in front look for the 'hole' through which the path passes.

Bear left and cut the corner of the field so that the river is on your right. Leave the river and aim for the gap in the fence opposite, crossing a small stream, almost dry in summer, as you do so. Then bear right to an iron gate opposite where you will reach the lane that you left when walking the Taw upstream.

Almost opposite across the lane is a yellow arrow marker directing you into the next field. A very mellow, peaceful valley is ahead. Cross the field to a gated footbridge and stile over a stream. Bear left across the next field to the gate following the direction arrow.

Passing by on my summer's walk every footstep was marked by the crunch of snail shells - the remnants of a thrush's work. The ground was covered by a low stubble upon which hundreds of iridescent metallic green beetles battled for mates.

At the next gate bear left uphill to the ruined farm, its barn roof a corrugated iron sore vivid with rust. At the back of the barn is a long wooden feeding trough partly crushed where the wall has given way. The far end of the ruin is the cob-walled shell of a farmhouse embraced by a flourishing ivy.

From the farm keep the hedge on your left along a track and enter a wood. Keep straight on so that you remain above the Taw on your right and fir trees left. You will come to a gate and signpost pointing you through the plantation, part of the Tarka Trail. The path is narrow in places but easy to follow and mostly level.

After a gloomy stand of fir trees it runs through a clearing where in season pink speared foxgloves sway. Here one early summer's evening a lumbering grey shape padded across my path - a badger. We both started at each other's presence.

After a quarter of a mile or so leave the plantation by a gate, crossing directly over the next field to a stile and yellow arrow. Follow the arrowed sign left uphill but bear away from the hedge on your left until you reach the end of the hedge ending rather abruptly in the middle of the field. With this incomplete hedge now on your right walk to its end - the OS 1:50,000 map has the footpath turning to the north rather than continuing west - and in this instance the map should be ignored and the signs on the ground followed. At the path's end pass through a gate and turn left uphill onto a lane.

At the junction where the road meets Hawkridge Farm, turn right and follow the lane back to Nymet Rowland.

---

29. MID DEVON:
Countryside on Exeter's doorstep - 6 miles

Directions

Start: Stoke Woods, immediately north of Exeter.

Outline and
walk length: A gentle 6 miles of footpath, bridleway and a little road walking. An easy three hours depending on eagerness and refreshment breaks.

Getting there: At the roundabout junction of the A377 and A396 take the Wretford Lane turning which climbs a steep hill through a housing estate. At the top turn left.

Parking: Official car park on left in Stoke Woods.

Refreshments: Post office and general stores, and the Agricultural Inn, Brampford Speke. Post office and general stores, Stoke Canon Inn at Stoke Canon. Barton Cross Hotel Restaurant at Huxham Barton.

Map: OS 1:25,000 Exeter Pathfinder no. 1314 or OS 1:50,000 Exeter and Sidmouth, Landranger no. 192.

The open country laps at the edge of every town and village in Devon. The same is true of Exeter, where the broad-leaved and coniferous trees of Stoke Woods cloak its northern edge. In the floodplain below, the waters of the Exe and Culm mingle.

Leave Stoke Woods car park by the path in the bottom corner. Walk directly downhill. As the path bears left and levels out you will see it marked by a red banded wooden post. Some 150 yards further, where you meet a post marked with red and yellow bands, turn right and follow the path downhill. At the next "crossroads" of paths go straight over down to a broad stand of fir trees. At a T-junction of paths turn left following yellow banded wooden markers. The track is wide and falls gently between the fir trees. After a gate and stile there is a small car park and lane leading down to the A396. Where it meets the main road, turn right. The road is not particularly busy but care should be taken. After 3 minutes walking go left down a signposted bridleway and follow the track across the

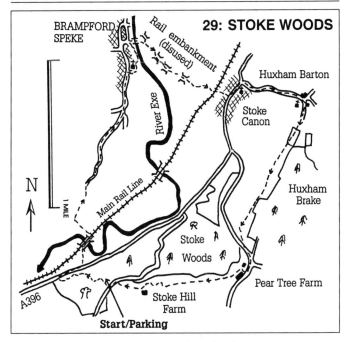

29: STOKE WOODS

BRAMPFORD SPEKE

Rail embankment (disused)

River Exe

Main Rail Line

N

1 MILE

Huxham Barton

Stoke Canon

Huxham Brake

Stoke Woods

Pear Tree Farm

A396

Stoke Hill Farm

Start/Parking

River Exe's floodplain up to the railway bridge.

Pale turquoise, pencil-lead thin dragonflies zigzag by, pursued by crayon thick, shiny metallic blue family members. The walker's crashing footfalls send them into wing-flickering flight before they come to rest just out of reach on another grassy stem. Here too the Exe is deep and sluggish, slothful in its summer senescence, a tired elder to the chattering youth who originally rushed off Exmoor. Its heavy green waters barely stir to the hiss and crackle of the power lines overhead. Breaking the stillness with a furious rumble, an Intercity 125 thunders past.

There is a walkway along the rail bridge where you can cross the Exe. At the far end a level crossing carries the walker over the rail line.

Walk along the track directly in front, across the meadow where sheep, cattle and a noisy gaggle of geese graze. At its end follow the footpath signed right, directing you diagonally over a grassy field over a stile and across another field in the middle of which another stile stands forlornly with no hedge or fence to carry the walker over. With farm buildings on your left, turn right along the lane. Follow it to its end, turning right up a short hill next to a very pretty cottage into Brampford Speke.

Pass the Agricultural Inn on your left and turn right towards St. Peter's Church. Having passed in front of the church and through an iron gate, follow the asphalted footpath between houses, eventually coming out near the village school. At this point turn sharp right, then left, descending from the river's bluff that you have been following, under a dilapidated footbridge, and back to the River Exe, crossing it via another wooden footbridge. The two houses to your left are the old railway station and stationmaster's house of the now disused and lifted branch line.

Now bear right, with the river on your right. The path shortly leaves the meadow and follows what used to be the old Exeter-Tiverton railway. In terms of views it's best to walk upon the embankment top until the path eventually bears off left to make a bee-line for Stoke Canon. Once again, the main railway line must be crossed, this time by a gated level crossing controlled by automatic barriers.

Once over, keep left - or depending how you look at it, straight on - into Stoke Canon. Turn left at the main road and then right past the Church of St. Mary Magdalene, whose main architectural gem is a Norman font hewn from a single block of lava. Follow the road over a couple of bridges that cross the River Culm and soon you will reach the tiny hamlet of Huxham Barton. Just past the Barton Cross Hotel Restaurant go right. You will pass the tiny Church of St. Mary on your right but keep straight on along a track. At its end go through the gate which is facing you and uphill with a stand of mature oaks on your right.

Here you have a choice at the top; if you go left then you will enter Huxham Brake wood over a stile and along a footpath; alternatively - and the better route - keep right under the mature oaks and through a metal gate and you will pass through the hedge onto an official bridleway. Here the walking is open and, while the high hedge does limit views over the Exe, there are fine views north

A sun-splashed Horsham Steps. (Walk 34)

Isolated Wistman's Wood on the River West Dart (Walk 36) *(author)*
The West Okement downstream of Lints Tor (Walk 39) *(author)*

up the River Culm valley. The bridleway passes briefly through a small wood before it curves to the left and joins the Stoke Hill road.

Turn left uphill onto this road. Ignore two lanes immediately on your left before turning right down an unsignposted bridleway, after Drew's Clieve Kennels and before Pear Tree Farm.

This bridleway climbs the ridge above Stoke Woods. Churned up when wet by horses, and ankle crackingly rutted when dry it provides brilliant views across the Exe to the opposing hills and is one of the walk's highlights. Pass Stoke Hill Farm via a gate, keeping the farm on your left, walk along the now surfaced bridleway enjoying the final sights before dropping back to Pennsylvania Road, turning left, and very shortly arrive back at the start.

---

30. MID DEVON:
Exploring the Teign Gorge from Drewsteignton - 6.5 miles

Directions

Start:	Drewsteignton village just inside the northern edge of Dartmoor and south of the A30.
Outline and walk length:	Along the lip of the Teign Gorge and its foot. Two routes - the longer, dropping into the Teign Gorge and including a couple of climbs, is 6.5 miles; the shorter loop which does not drop down to Fingle Bridge is a gentle 2 miles. Allow three hours.
Getting there:	Follow signs from the A30 to Drewsteignton.
Parking:	Limited parking in the village square near the church.
Refreshments:	Various at Fingle Bridge, but highlight is the Drewe Arms in village.
Map:	OS 1:25,000 Dartmoor; Outdoor Leisure no. 28.

Drewsteignton and the nearby Teign Gorge are a magnet for visitors. The Teign has cut a gorge 400-600 feet deep as it leaves Dartmoor and at Fingle Bridge a picturesque packhorse bridge crosses its rushing waters.

The gorge is heavily wooded and most visitors set out to walk a round route from Fingle Bridge which tends to become choked in summer. A

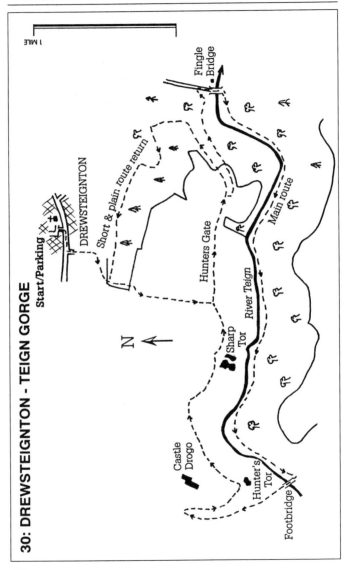

30: DREWSTEIGNTON - TEIGN GORGE

Start/Parking

DREWSTEIGNTON

1 MILE

N

Short & plain route return

Hunters Gate

River Teign

Main route

Sharp Tor

Castle Drogo

Hunter's Tor

Footbridge

Fingle Bridge

refreshing alternative is to begin the walk from Drewsteignton.

A white-walled cob, granite and thatch village, there are two places in Drewsteignton not to be missed.

The first is the fine granite Church of the Holy Trinity. Built in the late 15th and early 16th centuries, its amusing church guide is one of the most interesting of the genre and well worth searching out. From 1792-3 it details the sums paid for the killing of vermin - defined as badgers, foxes and the fearsome hedgehog! At the same time it notes that a feud amongst the singers had curtailed singing in the church over the previous 12 months. Well we all know how hunting hedgehog can divide communities.

The second place not to be missed is the Drewe Arms, where Mabel Mudge - 'Aunty' Mabel to all callers - was for seventy-five years the licensee, retiring at the grand old age of 99 in 1994. The pub once took in guests but is still at the time of writing a simple, smoky-ochre-walled tap room with basic trestle tables.

And so to the off. Leave Drewsteignton with the main square and church on your left, turning right at the junction. Follow this lane a short way, noting the last red brick building on the left, which used to be the village telegraph and old post office.

Just beyond, and signposted, turn left down a fairly steep track, with allotments immediately on your right. The track, after a turn to the right, drops to a small brook. Once over it, you surmount the hill opposite under woodland, crossing a stile and walking straight ahead with a boundary fence right. After cresting the ridge you will come to the lip of the gorge, not a mile from Drewsteignton.

Turn left and east along what is called Hunters Gate. Ahead are the bare rock-strewn flanks of Prestonbury Iron Age hillfort. Where the path divides, left is the short walk's return through deciduous and later coniferous trees, that runs back to the brook crossed earlier, shortly upon leaving Drewsteignton.

If you can, though, take the longer route - it will be rewarding. Take the right fork in the path that descends down to a lane onto which turn right to Fingle Bridge.

Cross the old packhorse bridge, which without resorting to too many cliches is simply lovely. When in leaf the trees shroud the river's course and soften the ravine's edges, while in winter their barren angular branches make the valley seem harsh and desolate.

Once upon the opposite bank, turn right, following the river upstream under thick foliage, catching occasional glimpses of the near sheer valley side opposite. The river swarms by. Passing a squat concrete building you are likely to hear a busy hum - the operation of one of only a handful of hydro-electric stations in Devon.

The path hugs the river only to be separated from it by a wide high granite blocked wall for the last few hundred yards up to a narrow metal footbridge on the right. Cross the Teign to the opposite bank. Walkers parked at Fingle Bridge return via the path downstream but you should leave the gorge by a footpath that is part of the Two Moors Way.

Passing a house, left, the path runs away from the river through a gate onto a driveway and then almost directly back upon itself right, onto a grassy path, this time curving back towards the gorge while still climbing.

Glimpsed through a fringe of Scots pines is Castle Drogo. The last castle to be built in Britain it was designed by Sir Edwin Lutyens at the behest of landowner Julius Drewe who bought the estate in 1910. The castle's building was suspended during the First World War and then scaled down as costs ran out of control. Finally completed in 1931 Mr Drewe had only five years to enjoy its granite austerity before he died in 1936. Castle Drogo's forbidding walls dominate the entrance to the Teign Gorge. The National Trust became its owners in 1974.

The path climbs through heathland before taking a sharp left and you will be confronted by the full incision the Teign has made in cutting its gorge. Standing above Hunter's Tor here is one of my favourite views in Devon.

The sandy path runs ahead along the valley's side towards a rocky outcrop, Sharp Tor, an easel stop for artists, with treeless moorland framed in the distant west; rough fields and farmsteads between. Shortly after Sharp Tor you are back at the point where the route first met the gorge.

You may retrace those same steps, or go on to complete a full round by including the shorter loop as described earlier.

```
31. MID DEVON:
Hidden charms of Newton St. Cyres and Whitestone Wood -
7 miles
```

Directions

Start:	Newton St. Cyres, just west of Exeter.
Outline and walk length:	A little under 7 miles of field, track and lane walking. Allow about four hours.
Getting there:	Newton St. Cyres is 4 miles from Exeter, the A377 running through it, and there is a regular bus service.
Parking:	In Newton St. Cyres turn left after the Crown and Sceptre pub and left again into a free car park.
Refreshments:	Crown and Sceptre, plus general stores in Newton St. Cyres. The Beer Engine pub a little further away at Sweetham (not on walk).
Map:	OS 1:25,000 Exeter. Unfortunately the walk is split across sheets 191 and 192 at the 1:50,000 scale.

Classic Devon combe country with high hills reaching 750 feet stretches west from Exeter to the very fringe of Dartmoor. Look at the OS map south of Crediton and you will see these sparsely populated hills bound by the River Yeo in the north and the A30 in the south. Narrow lanes, occasional farms and rare footpaths present the walker with few decent routes.

This walk climbs through the fields, deep natural woods and plantations of Whitestone, south of Newton St. Cyres. It reaches the high point of this particular range of hills before following a ridge east which offers excellent views over Exeter itself and down the Exe Estuary to distant Dawlish Warren.

Before leaving Newton St. Cyres call in at the Church of St. Cyre. The Northcote Monument dominates the church. It was erected in 1637 by Sir John, the son, in honour of Sir John, his father. Sir John senior appears life size, in full armour, with sword and foot planted firmly on a skull. Around the oval face of one of his wives is a terse sentence bemoaning her inability to produce more than one child - truly an unreconstructed squire. Also of interest is the delicate marquetry on the underside of the pulpit roof.

From the church retrace your steps to the lane and turn right. Walk out of Newton St. Cyres past a number of thatched cottages. During my visit a dilapidated Morris Eight was terminally parked by the roadside, acting as a prop for a flourishing yew tree.

Follow the road round to the right and uphill. You may wish to follow a footpath which runs across the fields left , but in the past I have found it variously ploughed up and barbed-wired over.

If the prospect of a difficult passage is unenticing carry on uphill, turning left at the crossroads and passing Woodley Farm along the lane that the footpath joins. After which, where the lane forks, keep left to the next junction, where a mildly overgrown footpath bears off on your right to a stile and into a small field.

Ahead are the combes of Whitestone Wood clad in oak, beech, birch, and

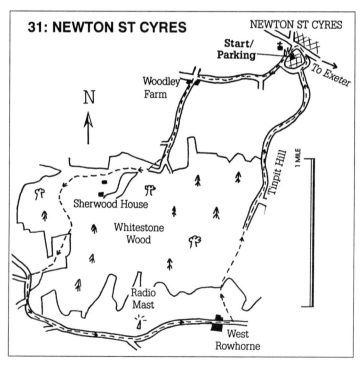

sombre conifers. In the fields above is the abrupt angular shape of the radio mast that you will pass later.

The path follows the hedge right to a stile, into a small wood in which I counted a quite amazing two dozen pheasants in the space of a few yards, their fate the not so distant crack of gunshot from nearby. On rejoining the lane go right, following it round first to the left then right. On your right you will come to a signposted footpath that drops back into the wood to follow a small stream, upstream. The wood lush with autumn rains, heavy with vapour, is deep and silent. The path is at all points clear to follow though not wide and you may expect it to disappear into an impenetrable thicket, which, aside from the occasional fallen tree thatched with moss, it happily does not do.

Interestingly you will come upon a stone pedestal on the right, just after which on the left and 'bleeding' down the hillside is a mass of broken bottles, stoneware, and plates, including bits of late 19th century marmalade jars. Presumably this is a local dump produced up the hill by Sherwood House and its cottages, before the municipal refuse collector had been invented.

Soon afterwards the path, with the brook still for company, passes through a chicken wire gate, and fence, another 'luxury' provided for the pheasants; it then enters a clearing with conifers to the left. Carry straight on, then bearing left uphill following the direction of a waymarking yellow arrow. Upon reaching the forestry track turn left then right again, arrowed up a narrow path between the trees. The path weaves back and forth but always climbs. It crosses a track and upon reaching another, turn right, again arrowed up to a junction, where you should go right up a not immediately obvious grassy path. Careful map reading is needed here as mistakes are easy.

On passing through a gate you are at last free from the cloak of trees. A sky of blunt prowed clouds and set against a vivid blue, empty of rain, is your reward - well maybe. Follow the hedge right through a field of yellowed grasses, then between two hedges, and gate turning left onto the lane.

The walk's climb is over. Now for the glory of the ridge. Follow the lane round, bearing left at the junction signposted to Whitestone Church and Exeter. At the next junction go left again.

Thatched cottages and ford at Newton St Cyres - the measuring board on the right gives an idea of how deep the Shuttern Brook may flow in flood

From this long ridge the views are simply wonderful. Looking north, the hills of Mid Devon amble to the fringes of Exmoor. South are the Haldon Hills, glimpses of Dartmoor, and east Exeter at the head of its estuary. The cathedral is prominent, as is Devon and Exeter Hospital with its ugly grey rectangular superstructure.

Having followed the lane along the ridge, at the next junction go left, passing the radio mast while walking downhill. On passing Rowhorne Farm and then West Rowhorne, and before reaching the next couple of Rowhornes, go left, signposted as a bridleway and marked with blue arrows. The next stage involves a gate, skirting round the top of a field, two gates, another field, and gate into Newton Wood. It is all downhill from here. Ignore all paths off left and right, including the sign to the Keeper's Cottage on the right. The track becomes a lane and where it forks go left into Newton St. Cyres, passing a huddle of picturesque thatched cottages, footbridge and ford over the Shuttern Brook.

---

32. NORTH DARTMOOR:
Leading the hound by the nose - Hound Tor and Bowerman's Nose - 4.5 miles

---

Directions

Start:	Car park below Hound Tor south of Manaton, near Bovey Tracey.
Outline and walk length:	An easy 4.5 miles on the edge of the moor with easy to follow paths and lanes. The route can be walked in a couple of hours but it is worth allowing longer because of the interest on the way.
Getting there:	Follow the signs to Hound Tor from the B3344 Bovey Tracey to Manaton road or from the Haytor to Widecombe in the Moor road.
Parking:	Car park below Hound Tor.
Refreshments:	There is usually an ice cream van at Hound Tor car park, otherwise none on walk.
Map:	OS 1:25,000 Dartmoor; Outdoor Leisure no. 28.
	Taking a compass wouldn't hurt, but you would have to work pretty hard to become lost.

Hound Tor is a mass of granite slabs and boulders in two distinct piles divided by a central avenue. It is justifiably considered one of the most striking and popular tors on Dartmoor. The summit commands impressive views to the even more popular Haytor Rocks due east and in a panoramic sweep to Honeybag and Chinkwell Tors, with the whale-back of Hameldon behind in the west.

Due north you may see rough mounds of granite boulders in nearby fields. These boulders used to be scattered across the hillside like those below Hound Tor itself. They slid down during brief periods of summer thaw when the moor, as the rest of southern England, was under periglacial conditions during the last Ice Age. The collective term for these granite blocks wherever they are found on Dartmoor is clitter. In recent years many farmers have hauled them from their ancient resting places so as to clear the way for fertilisers and other 'goodies' to improve the pasture, thereby irrevocably changing the nature of the moorland landscape.

Below Hound Tor are the remains of a medieval village and Greator Rocks, both worth a diversion. Excavated some years ago the village has revealed some interesting details about its medieval life - including early closing on Tuesdays and Thursdays - until AD 1349 when the Black Death ensured all day closing, every day, to the present.

Rather curiously Greator is grassed and vegetated partly up its flanks, and even on its top, as if like a late riser struggling with the bed covers, it is still to shrug off its blanket of soil.

Leave the car park and walk uphill to Hound Tor from where a broad grassy path falls between the medieval village (left) and Greator Rocks (right). Follow the path uphill, keeping Greator on your right, to a gate. After the gate the path descends, with woodland on your left, to a small granite bridge across Becka Brook under a hazel grove. The path bears right between silver birch trees and then left, keeping a low granite wall on the left. Looking back, the old

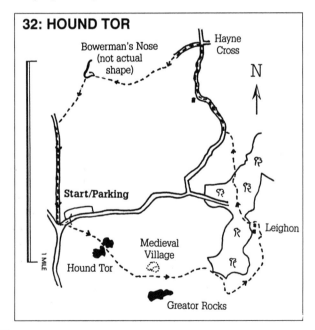

32: HOUND TOR

Bowerman's Nose
(not actual shape)

Hayne Cross

N

Start/Parking

1 MILE

Hound Tor

Medieval Village

Leighon

Greator Rocks

Bowerman's Nose with Easdon Tor beyond

quarry below Holwell Tor, its spoil heap crumbling towards the valley, is a notable local landmark.

The path is now a bridleway and runs gently downhill between walls to a small stand of houses called Leighon, which you should pass east of, still gently descending, possibly with squabbling squirrels for company. The path or track becomes metalled and you should see a painted yellow spot just before a private driveway. This marks a footpath that you follow over a number of stiles through a small wood. The path eventually leads into a grassy field and you keep roughly to the left-hand edge.

Having passed through a second field you will join, via a stile, a lane onto which you turn right. While it is hardly an A-road you should be aware of traffic, especially if you are walking with children.

Having passed a cluster of houses on your left, you will come to Hayne Cross crossroads, where you turn left, signposted to Hayne. The lane is at first metalled and then becomes a track, winding steadily uphill between stands (when fully grown) of bracken onto Hayne Down and its most notable feature at its north-west end, Bowerman's Nose.

The ridge offers views to Lustleigh Cleave opposite, down the valley to Bovey Tracey, to the north Cosdon, and of course, south to Hound Tor. The 'nose' of Bowerman cannot be seen from all angles, but it is clear from some, jutting out from near the top of this lone stack of granite. And it is, of course, like the flowers round about, not for picking.

The return is a short affair. You should cross the Down to the road below, turning left to follow it back towards Hound Tor and the car park.

---

33. NORTH DARTMOOR:
Prehistory on the moorland fringe - Gidleigh, Kestor Rock and the River Teign - 5.5 miles

---

Directions

Start:	Gidleigh, a tiny hamlet nestling in the lee of northern Dartmoor, about 3 miles west of Chagford.
Outline and walk length:	An easy 5.5 miles depending how far you wander exploring the prehistoric remains, along footpaths, lanes and some open moor. Allow two to three hours including one stiff climb.
Getting there:	From the A382 Moretonhampstead Road or from Chagford follow the signs to Gidleigh.
Parking:	In Gidleigh where parking is limited, so it is best to avoid the busiest periods. Or at the official car park at Scorhill above Berrydown, in which case you will have to turn right out of the car park's entrance to the walk's start at Gidleigh or alternatively walk the route in reverse.
Refreshments:	None in Gidleigh or on the walk. A pub, the Northmore Arms, is on the road to Whiddon Down.
Map:	OS 1:25,000 Dartmoor; Outdoor Leisure no. 28.

Before leaving Gidleigh visit its small beautifully maintained granite Church of the Holy Trinity. Note the barrel-like oak vaulting in the ceiling, and the painted and roughly-carved rood screen separating the altar and choir from the main body of the church.

The churchyard is unusual in Britain for being divided by a stream. Without wishing to sound ghoulish I find something fascinating about wandering round graveyards trying to discern some sense from the often bland, occasionally cryptic or humorous memorial epitaphs. Thumb-nail sketches of the dead. At Gidleigh, the Vogwells seem to qualify as local 17th century worthies and landowners, their names picked out in red leaded paint.

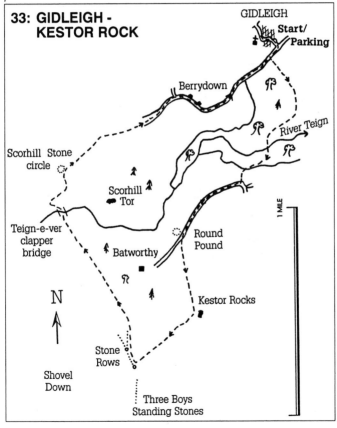

33: GIDLEIGH - KESTOR ROCK

GIDLEIGH
Start/Parking

Berrydown

River Teign

Scorhill Stone circle

Scorhill Tor

Teign-e-ver clapper bridge

Batworthy

Round Pound

Kestor Rocks

N

Stone Rows

Shovel Down

Three Boys Standing Stones

1 MILE

Gidleigh Castle dates from 1324 and can be spied through the bars of an iron gate. A small "keep", probably once with a low pitched lead covered roof, is now in the sort of picturesque ruinous condition that sent Victorian printers reaching for their etching plates.

To begin the walk turn round 180 degrees from the keep and walk along the road to its end; turn right uphill and then left where signposted to Kestor. Once over the stile you should have a broad track in front marked periodically by low yellow posts with a wood to the right.

This is the Mariners Way. Reputedly sailors who were too late to catch their ships from Dartmouth had the unenviable task of tramping across Devon to Bideford, where belatedly they might catch their ship when it put in to take on extra cargo before making sail across the Atlantic.

Bluebells carpet the woodland floor in spring and woodpeckers can be heard hammering out their homes among the trunks.

The path falls through a small but dense stand of coniferous trees before it widens as it enters oak woodland. Cross the North Teign by a footbridge over great boulders, round which the water starved river slips quietly in summer but roars after a downpour. Up the opposite bank is a stiff climb known locally as Glassy Steps, at the top of which turn right. Then go over a stile and turn right onto what is the asphalted road leading to Batworthy and the open moor.

Follow the road until you reach the low stone walls of Round Pound then strike off left uphill for Kestor Rocks.

Kestor is a fine pile of rocks, allowing clear views to the wild north moor and east down the Teign valley. Its best known feature is its rock basin, 30 inches deep and up to 3 feet wide. Antiquaries of the last century felt it had to be man-made - associated with some bizarre Druidic ritual, the nature of which was probably too horrible to contemplate.

Reality is a little more prosaic. The Druids never inhabited Dartmoor. The basin was, and still is, being cut into the tor's summit by the processes of freeze thaw and chemical erosion.

But the evidence of very real prehistoric settlement is all around. Excavations of Round Pound have revealed it as an Iron Age metalworkers' hut but more fascinating is the complex of double stone rows and a very rare fourfold stone circle near Batworthy Corner.

Scramble down from the tor and head south-west onto Shovel

Down towards the series of stone rows and Three Boys standing stones which can easily be seen from the summit.

Leaving the stones behind, turn back to Batworthy and follow the walled field edge for about a third of a mile north-west down to the River Teign, which can be crossed by the Teign-e-ver clapper bridge. Small children should probably be shepherded across the two uneven granite slabs that pass for a bridge over a narrow swiftly-flowing part of this river.

One of Dartmoor's most beautiful places, this short stretch of the Teign is fortunately off the main visitors' trail so it never becomes overwhelmed by picnickers.

Grey wagtails dart along the river, and as the evening shadows lengthen that rare of birds, the dipper, can be seen bobbing from rock to rock, plunging into the waterfalls in search of insects and larvae.

Just down from the clapper lies the Teign Tolmen, allegedly a cure for whooping cough, rheumatism and various other ailments.

Over many thousands of years this large boulder has been worn away into a ring by storm water swirling stones and gravel upon its surface. Now a hole 2 to 3 feet wide and 4 feet deep has been cut right through to the river bottom.

For the moderately nimble it is still possible to slide down, passing through the boulder - and receiving your cure - but beware if the river level is up - you are liable to get wet.

Leaving the river to its helter-skelter rush to the sea, trace the track that leads up to the impressive stone circle of Scorhill, the largest stone of which stands a lofty 8 feet high.

The influence of magic and superstition in the history of Dartmoor is never far away. It is said that a fickle or suspect wife underwent a test to prove her virtue, that involved washing in Cranmere Pool, running three times around Scorhill Circle, passing through the Teign Tolmen and then praying for forgiveness while kneeling in front of the great standing stones at Grey Wethers, near Fernworthy (visited in Walks 37 and 40).

If her virtue was not proved then the stone would grimly fall slowly forward, crushing her. Visitors to Grey Wethers would be misguided to draw comfort from finding all the stones upright - as all had fallen, prior to their restoration at the turn of this century!

The final leg back to Gidleigh is quite straightforward. From Scorhill Circle follow the track over Scorhill Down. The track leaves the moor between walled fields running to Scorhill car park. At the road bear right down the metalled lane past Berrydown to Gidleigh.

---

34. NORTH DARTMOOR:
From sleepy Lustleigh to wild Lustleigh Cleave
via Horsham Steps - 7 miles

Directions

Start:	Lustleigh between Bovey Tracey and Moretonhampstead on the eastern edge of Dartmoor.
Outline and walk length:	Mostly easy walking with moderate climbs in and around the delightful wooded Lustleigh Cleave. Along footpaths with a little lane walking, some 7 miles in all. Allow three to four hours.
Getting there:	Off the A382 Moretonhampstead-Bovey Tracey road, follow the signs to Lustleigh.
Parking:	In the centre of Lustleigh around the church, which can be very limited during the peak visitor season.
Refreshments:	The Cleave Inn, Primrose Tearooms and general stores in Lustleigh, plus the Kestor Inn and general store in Water.
Map:	OS 1:25,000 Dartmoor; Outdoor Leisure no. 28.

Lustleigh deserves inclusion in any guide on the grounds of its attractive mixture of ancient thatched cottages and Victorian grand houses and artisan terraces. And then of course there is nearby Lustleigh Cleave. The village is the sort of place where you settle down for 40 post-lunch winks only to wake up 80 winks later in early evening - a village that is not so much sleepy as comatose.

At its centre is the 13th century parish Church of St. John the Baptist, planted in a raised Saxon oval graveyard that dates back to the 5th or 6th century.

Around the church are a number of whitewashed thatched cottages. These were originally labourers' cottages for the employees of the farm that is now the Cleave Inn. The embankment and bridges behind them used to carry the now dismantled railway line that ran between Newton Abbot and

Moretonhampstead.

One sultry summer's morning, unable to stir myself from a church bench, I chatted with an 82-year-old local man. Had he seen many changes in the last eighty or so years? "Ooh some," he replied, "people change, houses stay the same." Before contradicting himself by pointing to all the buildings he had helped build including the Primrose Cottage Tea Rooms opposite.

Leave Lustleigh by passing the general store and keeping the row of red brick terraced houses on your right. Walk downhill passing over a small brook.

The road starts uphill past a chapel where you should turn right. There are assorted houses set back from the road on your left and shortly you will come to a steep road on your left which you should take.

This road winds between a number of substantial Victorian

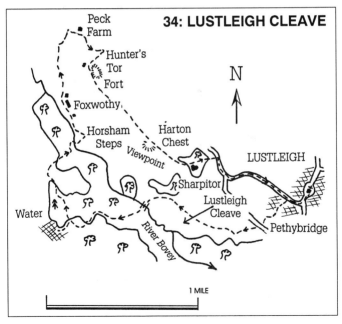

dwellings before cresting a hill amid a stand of thatched cottages, an old hamlet called Pethybridge. Just past Pethybridge, turn left downhill then almost immediately right still on the road, and then left at the track and bridleway straight in front of you. This runs uphill past Waye Cottage and once through a gate the descent into Lustleigh Cleave begins.

Do not be tempted by paths to the left signposted to Hisley. Keep walking gently downhill bearing right, finally following the footpath signposted to Manaton via Water.

As autumn wears on the tree canopy sheds its dressing of leaves, exposing the valley to sight. But during summer a thick canopy allows in only dancing shadows and a thin cooling breeze.

One afternoon I walked this path on a hot clear summer's day and was completely baffled by the light patter of what sounded like rain. As I walked on so the sound increased until I stumbled over two enormous ants' nests. Ants were streaming from them, climbing two nearby silver birch trees and from the branches a good number were raining down across the surrounding vegetation - tightening my collar I beat a hasty retreat.

Shortly the path turns left and descends to the River Bovey which it crosses by the medium of a bridge fashioned from two tree trunks and a supporting handrail. Now in thick woodland the path climbs towards the hamlet of Water.

The path climbs steadily under thick mature woodland and at one point becomes the bed of an infant stream. At its top turn right for the main route or continue straight on behind the farm buildings which will bring you to the ancient tranquil hamlet of Water - really a must for a visit. If refreshments are required walk to the road's end and turn right for the Kestor Inn.

Retracing your steps rejoin the track behind the farm buildings. If you are coming from Water this will now mean a left turn. The path is now a well defined track running between stands of coniferous trees.

You should turn right where signposted to Horsham Steps. The path runs past a "chocolate box" cottage before dipping under tall oaks. The path descends to Horsham Steps which are found just upstream from a large, almost still pool, on the River Bovey.

At the Steps, the Bovey, its bed choked with boulders, squeezes between the joints. The boulders continue for some way upstream and a good time

Lustleigh

can be spent leaping around tracing the river's main channel. Like the more famous Becky Falls nearby, Horsham Steps is impressive in flood.

Cross to the opposite bank. The path leaves the river and comes to a junction where you should go left. Skirt Foxworthy Mill - now a domestic house - bearing right onto a concrete driveway which runs in front of Foxworthy - complete with a most impressive granite cottage at its western end. You will begin to climb as you bear right up a signposted bridleway. This is the Cleave's mouth and the path rises for half a mile.

Look to turn right to Peck Farm and start the ascent of the Cleave's summit ridge.

At the top a small tor, Hunter's Tor, is accompanied by the low banks of a prehistoric fort. The heather covered ridge is barren and windswept providing fine views of the Cleave, but also north and west to Cosdon Beacon, Steeperton Tor, North Bovey village and Manaton House Hotel.

Looking south and south-west Haytor and its disused quarries, Hound Tor and Bowerman's Nose all rear into sight. Soon though a crisp wind will spur you along the ridge. A massive perched boulder, Harton Chest, part way along the ridge is worth scrambling onto. Be careful because its exposed position which gives it such excellent views up and down the

Cleave also means it has long drops on three sides.

Cross the top of the ridge and the path soon returns to the shelter of woodland, in which you will pass Sharpitor and Nutcrackers.

The Nutcrackers rock was once a huge rocking or logan stone used by Lustleigh villagers to - surprise, surprise - crack nuts, but now unfortunately broken. Last century it was cast from its delicate balance by an army officer - more intent on displaying his brawn than brain to a local lovely.

Where the path descends to a road turn right. Thereafter take the first left. This will bring you onto the road that leads past the chapel and so shortly back to Lustleigh.

---

35. NORTH DARTMOOR:
Belstone Common south to Steeperton Tor returning down the River Taw. Ridge and river 7.5 miles.

Directions

Start:	Belstone, just inside the northernmost edge of the Dartmoor National Park.
Outline and walk length:	A 7.5 mile ridge and river route with some stiff walking, taking four to five hours - the return leg is all level.
Getting there:	Follow the A30 Okehampton road turning onto its old course at Whiddon Down or Okehampton then signs to Belstone.
Parking:	Drive into Belstone but rather than turning into the village proper, keep right passing the post office. Follow the road signposted as 'No through road' uphill which quickly becomes a track. At its end there is a small car park opposite a South West Water treatment works.
Refreshments:	In Belstone a pub, the Tors, as well as a post office and shop. None on the walk.
Map:	OS 1:25,000 Dartmoor; Outdoor Leisure no. 28.
Warning:	Part of the route runs through the Okehampton Army Firing Range. If a red flag is flying over the range firing is in progress. Firing dates and times, which include night firing, are given in many local papers. To be certain no firing is taking place telephone the range information line on Exeter 70164/Okehampton 52939/Plymouth 501478/Torquay 294592, or the daily update on (01837) 52241/41 extension 3210, before you set out.

Belstone is an unusual Dartmoor village. Thatched roofs are replaced by slate which combined with the rather sombre well-cut granite of the house walls creates an air of particular solidity, no doubt satisfying the turn of the century middle classes who caused its expansion.

The village has retained its stocks, set in the small green on the left as you turn into the village.

Outside the post office an old 'Telegraph Office' sign hangs.

Belstone sits at the mouth of broad grassy Taw Marsh. Immediately south-east is the bluff bear's back of Cosdon Beacon at 1799 feet. But the scene is dominated by the deceptively mountainous looking Steeperton Tor guarding the head of Taw Marsh.

The walk is simplicity itself. An easy to follow ridge and river route with fine views of the north moor. The route follows the western ridge over Belstone Common and Oke Tor to Steeperton Tor, returning along the Taw.

On leaving the small car park follow the track uphill passing through the gate that leads to Watchet Hill and the open moor. Immediately strike out uphill for the flagpole, noticing on the way a small stone circle called the Nine Stones or Nine Maidens.

The next port of call is Belstone Tor (1568 feet) which is broken into a series of quite separate tors. As you ascend so the north moor will open out all around, with High Willhays and Yes Tor, Dartmoor's highest points, doing their best to tower. Beyond Belstone Tor continue along the ridge as it curves round to the fortress-like Oke Tor.

The tors that make up Belstone are well worth scrambling up and can be consequently considered 'bagged'. On climbing the third and highest of the pile, the basin of the River Taw and its marsh will be in view, and above it the triangular and impressive Steeperton Tor, the walk's halfway point.

Beyond the last of the Belstone tors you will cross the tumbledown 'Irishman's Wall', a failed 19th century attempt to enclose Belstone Common at a time when 'improving' the quality of the moor was very much in vogue.

Under iron-clad skies with winds howling, this is a wild place but as long as you remain upon the ridge there is no fear of lost bearings.

After dropping down a little, the route climbs to Oke Tor just south of which is one of many military tracks that criss-cross and blight this part of the moor. Follow the track which runs broadly in

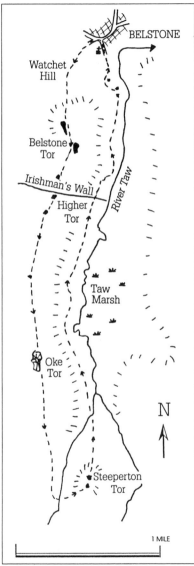

BELSTONE

Watchet
Hill

Belstone
Tor

Irishman's Wall

Higher
Tor

River Taw

Taw
Marsh

Oke
Tor

N

↑

Steeperton
Tor

1 MILE

35: BELSTONE - STEEPERTON TOR

the direction of Steeperton and drops into the gorge, crossing the River Taw where it is little more than a stream.

It is possible to cross further downstream, but this makes for a particularly exacting climb of Steeperton and so it is best to approach the tor from the southwest, which you do by immediately leaving the track once across the Taw and climbing left uphill.

As a tor, Steeperton is preciously short of granite outcrops. What there is, has had an army observation post built into it, which while worth bemoaning as part of the military use of Dartmoor generally, is an absolute boon in bad weather because the tor can be ferociously exposed.

In good weather, though, it is a place as benign as any other on the moor and blessed with particularly fine views downstream over the broad plain of Taw Marsh. The bluff shape of Cosdon Beacon can also be seen, itself a worthy return route to Belstone for the fit and eager. Due south the ground rises gently to the featureless heart of the moor and an area for those with accomplished map and compass skills.

The return leg is quite straightforward. Walk directly down Steeperton, heading due north and towards the broad basin that is Taw Marsh. You should look to cross Steeperton Brook onto the left bank before it joins the Taw, so that when the Taw unites the two streams the river is on your right. The Taw is now your guide back to Belstone but it should not be religiously followed as it winds through some very wet places, all the wetter for the mounds thrown up by the tinners just north of where the Taw is joined by the Steeperton Brook. Instead, look to keep to the dry ground at the foot of the ridge you walked earlier. Part way along you will come to a track-cum-road which runs off the moor via a gate. The road lined with mature houses and trees returns to Belstone.

The valley bottom has a number of curiosities worth leaving the home-ward track to explore. Halfway along the valley floor are low flat-topped mounds in which man-hole covers are set, the sound of water hissing below. Two and a half million gallons of water is extracted daily from these shallow wells but the hope in the 1950s that the gravels of Taw Marsh were an enormous natural underground reservoir waiting to be tapped were dashed when high concentrations of radioactive radon gas were found in the water.

After a bright winter's day mist rises swiftly from the marsh, swallowing the land and leaving Steeperton a disembodied island in an ethereal inland sea.

---

36. NORTH DARTMOOR:
Ancient oaks and standing stones - Two Bridges, Wistman's Wood, the West Dart and Beardown Man. Ridge and river - 8 miles

---

Directions

Start: Two Bridges, between Postbridge and Princetown, central Dartmoor.

Outline and walk length: A ridge and river route 8 miles long. Highlights include ancient Wistman's Wood, seven tors and standing stone Beardown Man. Some boggy ground to cover, though much of route is fairly dry underfoot. Allow four to five hours.

Getting there:	Follow the B3212 transmoor road which leads directly to Two Bridges. Alternatively take the A38 turning off at Ashburton and following the signs to Princetown or the B3357 from Tavistock.
Parking:	In car park and disused quarry immediately west of Two Bridges and almost directly opposite the hotel.
Refreshments:	Two Bridges Hotel for pub food and beer, otherwise none on walk.
Map:	OS 1:25,000 Dartmoor; Outdoor Leisure no. 28. Take a compass.
Warning:	Part of the route passes through Merrivale Army Firing Range. If a red flag is flying over the range firing is in progress. Firing dates and times, which include night firing, are given in many local papers. To be certain no firing is taking place telephone the range information line on Exeter 70164/Okehampton 52939/Plymouth 501478/Torquay 294592, or the daily update on (01837) 52241/41 extension 3210, before you set out.

Wistman's Wood is a celebrated natural feature of Dartmoor. It is one of the last vestiges of high altitude oak woodland (the others being Black-a-tor Copse and Piles Corner) which used to cloak much of the moor before prehistoric man set about the land with his flint axe and fire.

Stunted wizened oaks creep from the cracks between great moss draped boulders. Writers of the last century marvelled at being able to touch the tops of even the tallest trees. Recent years though have witnessed a growth spurt and the boughs are taller now but no less fantastic in all their contortions.

Unsurprisingly for such an unusual natural curiosity the wood has given rise to many tales of the mysterious - indeed its name is probably a corruption of the Dartmoor vernacular "wisht" meaning haunted or pixie-led.

This walk is a ridge and river route and follows the West Dart upstream until Wistman's Wood from where it climbs the east bank to take in Longaford, Higher White and Lower White Tors, before crossing the West Dart and returning via Rough, Devil's and Beardown Tors along the west bank ridge.

Before leaving the car park just above Two Bridges, look closely at the small protected status quarry at the path's beginning. It is a particular calling place for geologists: in the quarry face there seems to be an infant

36: TWO BRIDGES

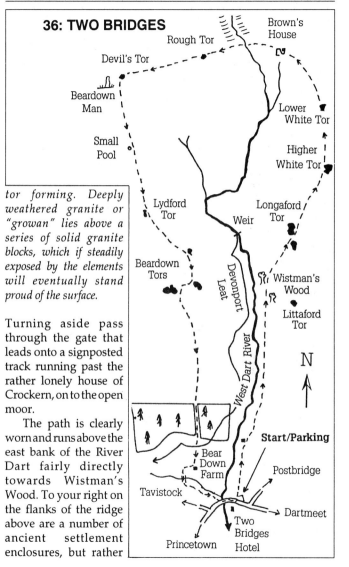

Brown's House

Rough Tor

Devil's Tor

Beardown Man

Small Pool

Lydford Tor

Weir

Longaford Tor

Lower White Tor

Higher White Tor

Beardown Tors

Devonport Leat

Wistman's Wood

Littaford Tor

West Dart River

N

tor forming. Deeply weathered granite or "growan" lies above a series of solid granite blocks, which if steadily exposed by the elements will eventually stand proud of the surface.

Turning aside pass through the gate that leads onto a signposted track running past the rather lonely house of Crockern, on to the open moor.

The path is clearly worn and runs above the east bank of the River Dart fairly directly towards Wistman's Wood. To your right on the flanks of the ridge above are a number of ancient settlement enclosures, but rather

Bear Down Farm

Tavistock

Start/Parking

Postbridge

Dartmeet

Two Bridges Hotel

Princetown

153

than visiting them you may wish to save your stamina for the trials to come.

After a mile or so you will reach the edge of Wistman's Wood. The path disappears under gnarled branches, but can be followed by tracing those granite blocks either polished smooth by footfall or where the carpet of moss is worn.

Wistman's is at its most captivating on fog laden days when dank and silent. Pearls of water become snared in great beards of lichen hanging from the branches.

Upon reaching a fence in the wood bear right uphill emerging from under the low canopy and head north-east for Longaford Tor on the ridge above.

Down in its marshy bottom the West Dart clatters on its way, its volume lessened by the water drawn off at a small weir feeding the Devonport Leat.

From Longaford Tor make for Higher White Tor, less than a quarter of a mile away to the north-east, and passing a stone row in the process.

From here there are fine views across to Hound Tor, Hameldon, Haytor Rocks and Bellever in the east, with the chimneys of Powder Mills (a disused gunpowder factory) in the foreground, and to the south the featureless bluff of the southern moor.

From Higher White Tor head for Lower White Tor, a low insignificant mound largely occupied by rabbits.

From here it should be possible to make out due north-west the outline of Brown's House, which, if ever completed, would probably have been the farmstead of one of Dartmoor's early 19th century settlers.

Brown's House marks the most northerly point of the walk and you should now turn west and make for the West Dart, crossing it just downstream of its exit from a small narrow valley. Then climb directly uphill, making for Rough Tor and its Merrivale Range noticeboard.

It is one of the idiosyncrasies of Dartmoor that as you climb uphill the ground underfoot becomes steadily wetter, as if the spongy moor is only reluctantly drained. Around here you will find that water-proofing precautions taken in anticipation of boggy ground pay off.

Confronted by a stretch of open moorland at Rough Tor, you should make east-south-east for Devil's Tor.

View north from Longaford Tor

Should you lose your bearings in bad weather, turn south. If you have missed the ridge which is the return route, you should at worst find yourself walking down what will turn into the River Cowsic which leads back to Two Bridges.

Bad weather aside, Devil's Tor is less than half a mile from Rough Tor and clearly in sight. It is notable not in its own right but for Beardown Man, the 12 feet high standing stone nearby.

The tor itself is just high enough for the tired walker to slump down in its lee out of a serrating west wind, and watch the clouds plough by.

On leaving Devil's Tor, walk due south along the ridge, passing a small pool on the way, to Lydford Tor and so to the three impressive outcrops comprising Beardown Tors. In particular notice the large overhang at the base of one of the outcrops. The path here is permissive across Duchy of Cornwall estate land.

By now your limbs will be weary and so make directly for the coniferous plantation through which a broad track passes.

At its end cross a stile onto an official footpath which marked with yellow spots, skirts the outbuildings of Bear Down Farm, before crossing the Cowsic and running by its right bank back to Two Bridges.

---

37. NORTH DARTMOOR:
Ancient bridges and older waterfalls - Postbridge clapper bridge to East Dart waterfall via Grey Wethers and Sittaford Tor - 8 miles

---

Directions

Start:	Postbridge, central Dartmoor.
Outline and	
walk length:	The East Dart is the guide for most of the walk with a short stretch over open moorland. Allow four hours or so for the 8 miles and go prepared for the vagaries of Dartmoor weather.
Getting there:	Follow the B3212 across Dartmoor to Postbridge.
By bus:	Transmoor link, contact Devon General.
Parking:	Large National Park car park and information centre at the southern end of Postbridge.
Refreshments:	Various in Postbridge including pub and general stores, all very busy in high summer. None on walk.
Map:	OS 1:25,000 Dartmoor; Outdoor Leisure no. 28. Take a compass.
Warning:	While this walk does not cross into any of the Army ranges it does come close to the Merrivale and Okehampton ranges. In case you stray further up the East Dart check the firing times. If a red flag is flying over the range firing is in progress. Firing dates and times, which include night firing, are given in many local papers. To be certain no firing is taking place telephone the range information line on Exeter 70164/Okehampton 52939/Plymouth 501478/Torquay 294592, or the daily update on (01837) 52241/41 extension 3210, before you set out.

Where the East Dart flows past Postbridge it provides an excellent route through the shallow valleys and low rounded hills so typical of Dartmoor, to the high northern moor.

Famous for its clapper bridge, Postbridge is on most visitors' standard itinerary. Close by are a number of farms and old tenements of the ancient Royal Forest of Dartmoor but there is little in Postbridge proper to detain your boots.

Bellever Forestry Commission plantation lies immediately south so it follows logically that this walk goes north.

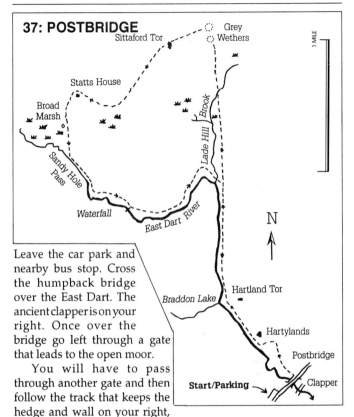

37: POSTBRIDGE

Grey Wethers

Sittaford Tor

1 MILE

Statts House

Broad Marsh

Lade Hill Brook

Sandy Hole Pass

Waterfall

East Dart River

N

Leave the car park and nearby bus stop. Cross the humpback bridge over the East Dart. The ancient clapper is on your right. Once over the bridge go left through a gate that leads to the open moor.

Hartland Tor

Braddon Lake

Hartylands

Postbridge

Start/Parking

Clapper

You will have to pass through another gate and then follow the track that keeps the hedge and wall on your right, round what is in effect two sides of a triangle. Many walkers instead make a bee-line across the open ground to where the wall meets the river.

Having reached this point you will now be walking upstream with the East Dart on your left; to your right the large house of Hartylands. Continuing upstream you will pass through another gate, just past which is a small but thick stand of what seems to be bamboo!

A hurrying small river, low willows draw life from the East Dart's cold waters. A willing if intellectually challenged labrador pursues pebbles tossed into the water, with soft plunging sounds, by its owner.

The path is clear to follow, alongside or through trouser snagging gorse. The East Dart is joined by a small stream, Braddon Lake, from the left, after which the valley narrows but the path is clear ahead.

Further on the valley broadens a little as the East Dart begins to loop back on itself to the left. At this point you should continue straight on, leaving the Dart and following a small tributary, Lade Hill Brook, though it is not named on the OS Outdoor Leisure series map. Keep the brook on your left.

Within a few yards of where the brook joins the East Dart there is a well preserved "beehive-hut" or tinners' cache amid the rubble of tin streaming. Alluvial deposits and later lodes near the surface, of cassiterite - tin ore - were mined on Dartmoor from the 12th century until the early to mid 17th century when the English Civil War brought the final collapse of the industry. Deep mining was to emerge later at the end of the 18th century. The "beehive" hut may seem today like a mound of broken granite, but this small low corbelled structure would have been used by the tinners to store ingots of tin or tools.

Continue to follow the brook upstream moving onto higher ground to avoid a boggy area below Sittaford Tor. If you keep straight on you will reach the impressive twin stone circles of Grey Wethers (see Walk 40). From Grey Wethers follow the nearby boundary wall uphill. After a short pull you will reach Sittaford, a rather low grassy tor not sure whether it is coming or going.

Below, a youthful River Teign flows between gloomy Fernworthy and the ruin of Teignhead Farm. Looking due west is the conical shape of Cut Hill, and north rolling heather and grass moor.

From Sittaford make your way due south-west along the ridge, going just south a little to avoid dropping down too much into the infant valley of the Little Varracombe brook, but all the time aiming for the ruin of Statts House on the top of Winney's Down. From here it is but a short drop south-west along the cutting or peat pass to a wide plain across which the East Dart flows, an area called Broad Marsh.

Do not be seduced into trying to cross this boggy area, instead keep to the dry ground above and skirt around it south, rejoining the East Dart on your right to walk downstream - but remaining above where it enters the surprisingly steep gorge of Sandy Hole

Pass; there are numerous sheep tracks to follow here.

In a past incarnation I managed to ignore both of the above pieces of advice. Having 'enjoyed' a fruitless half-hour retracing my steps through Broad Marsh I fell into a cunningly disguised bog on the right bank of Sandy Hole Pass itself and finally ended up in Postbridge on a blazing August day, looking as if I'd been bog-bungling with a hippo.

The exit from Sandy Hole is guarded by two outcrops of granite; having passed them you will soon hear, if it has recently been raining, the sound of thundering - well almost - water. In drier weather it's rather an apology for a waterfall over which the East Dart tumbles. Either way it's a most restful spot.

The return to Postbridge from here is simplicity itself. On the left bank of the East Dart with the river on your right there is the course of an old leat - now dry. This used to take water from just above the waterfall by a circuitous 8 mile journey to the tin mines at Birch Tor and Vitifer, near Warren house.

This you should follow, but where it turns northwards to skirt the steep cut made by Winney's Down Brook you leave it and more closely follow the river; shortly you will find yourself on a clear path that runs back to the point where you left the East Dart to follow Lade Hill Brook up to Sittaford Tor.

Turning right, all that remains is to retrace your steps to Postbridge.

---

38. NORTH DARTMOOR:
**The heart of the high moor - along the Tavy to Fur Tor.
Ridge and river - 9 miles.**

Directions

Start: Lanehead, 3 miles from Mary Tavy on the western edge of Dartmoor National Park between Okehampton and Tavistock.

*Outline and
walk length:*   A ridge and river route carrying the walker into the heart of the north moor. The main walk via Fur Tor is 9 miles. Allow five to six hours. It is quite demanding despite following the Tavy for most of the way and you should go prepared for typical Dartmoor bogginess and weather. Tavy Cleave is

mostly dry going but in a number of places you will have to scramble over clitter which can be particularly tricky when wet or icy. The shorter loop, including the Cleave, Hare and Ger Tors but excluding Fur Tor, is 4-5 miles long. It includes a stiff climb but is a glorious alternative for those who do not wish to penetrate too far into the moor. Allow two to three hours.

Getting there: Turn off the A386 at the northern end of Mary Tavy following signs first to Horndon then beyond to Lanehead.

Parking: Car park at Lanehead.

Refreshments: None on walk.

Map: OS Outdoor 1:25,000 Dartmoor; Outdoor Leisure no. 28. Take a compass.

Warning: This walk falls within the Willsworthy army range and the longer route also within the Okehampton army range. If a red flag is flying over the range firing is in progress. Firing dates and times, which include night firing, are given in many local papers. To be certain no firing is taking place telephone the range information line on Exeter 70164/ Okehampton 52939/Plymouth 501478/Torquay 294592, or the daily update on (01837) 52241/41 extension 3210, before you set out.

Tavy Cleave is one of Dartmoor's undisputed highlights. Angular Ger Tor guards its mouth while five unnamed, precipitous tors crumble into the River Tavy below, its foaming waters racing from the high fen round Fur Tor and Cut Hill. Tumbling in a series of small waterfalls, the Tavy glides across great slabs of granite and is trapped in broad sandy pools which reveal miniature beaches when the river level falls. Stunning all year round, autumn is probably the most exciting time to walk the cleave. Against a background of purple heather, curled grasses of yellow and browns 'burnt' with the first frosts, low mountain ash flourish their seasonal fruit.

Whether you choose the short or more demanding longer loop the outward leg via Tavy Cleave and return via Hare Tor are identical.

To start leave Lanehead and follow the track east towards Nattor Farm. Continue uphill past the farm to the Wheal Friendship leat, which used to power the copper mine of the same name near Horndon and now fills the Wheal Jewell reservoir. At the leat turn right and follow its course upstream.

The path is clearly defined and well trod. Round Nat Tor the leat picks up speed. At this point it is worth dropping down to the River Tavy itself, if you wish, to see Ger Tor in all its grandeur, towering above the cleave entrance, clitter spewed down its sides. Return to the leat.

Under Ger Tor the leat returns to its source and the walker gets some idea of how much water is drawn off from the river.

Crossing by a small footbridge by a low granite building there is a narrow but clearly defined footpath that runs more or less along the river's bank with the

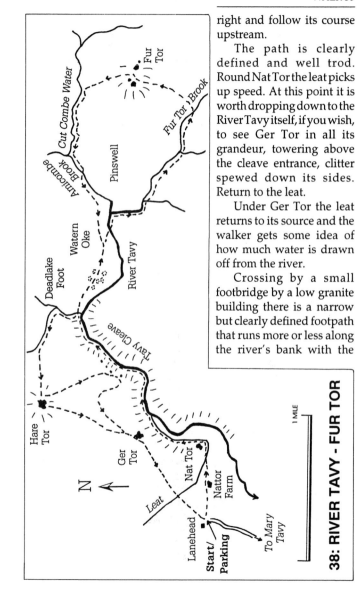

38: RIVER TAVY - FUR TOR

Tavy always on your right.

The river takes a sharp left as you enter the Cleave proper.

Here the river runs through a deep gorge out of which, towering chimney-like, five unnamed tors rise on the west side.

The river can look truly placid in summer as it falls over a series of small waterfalls with a gentle plunging sound but boulders in its bed 5 feet high and more attest to its storm force.

From the clitter-strewn cleave's side leaping with a softening beauty grow a few stunted mountain ash. The approach of autumn heralds their vivid red berries, a startling blossom which glows as the climbing sun parts the morning's shadows.

A breathtakingly beautiful place: the river pauses in wide sandy bottomed pools before continuing its passage to the sea; a journey that is so short and steep that the River Tavy rates as the second fastest flowing river in England.

All too soon though the gorge is passed at the point where the Tavy is joined by the Rattle Brook, descending from the north. It is here that the "short-loopers" turn left up Rattle Brook.

For those heading for Fur Tor, follow Rattle Brook a little upstream until a crossing point is found, then climb the short steep bank onto Watern Oke. Walk upstream parallel to but well above the Tavy, passing through a long set of hut circles as you do so. Below, a handful of stunted oaks cling to the river's edge.

Ahead rises extensive clitter-strewn Fur Tor. A large tor, its very size makes it unusual as larger tors tend to be found on the moor's edge, not its bleak heart.

Soon the walker has a difficult choice. Fur Tor almost cries out for a direct assault on its summit but, be warned, it is a slog. Pinswell is wet, with turf-ties to negotiate, and Fur Tor offers the walker a series of dispiriting false summits. The alternative is longer but drier - and here avoiding wet boots is the better part of valour.

After a broad marshy area, where a stream, the Western Red lake, joins the river from the south, the Tavy now little more than a stream itself passes through a narrow rocky channel. Here cross to the opposite bank before it is joined at the foot of Pinswell and Fur Tor by the Amicombe Brook at Sandy Ford.

Climb the bank so that you are upon the dry grassy ground above the Tavy, now on your left. Continue upstream crossing the Eastern Red Lake stream and then dropping down to cross the Tavy

Fur Tor with a light dusting of snow looking west. The Tavy is in the centre of the picture with Hare Tor beyond to the right

itself, using some old tinners' spoil heaps to avoid the majority of a boggy area. Now follow Fur Tor Brook upstream due south-east. Keep the brook on your left but remaining on the drier ground above it until you have passed the last of a wide boggy section. Only then strike due north having almost crested the ridge and reach Fur Tor from the south.

The main body of Fur Tor rock involves a testing scramble to its summit where undisturbed crows have nested in past years. The tor is one of the focal points for walkers on the north moor and letter-boxers are frequently found poking around its crevices hunting for that all important rubber stamp.

Weather permitting the summit views are magnificent: west back down the Tavy to Hare Tor with Bodmin Moor in the background; north to High Willhays looming over the broad trough where the West Okement flows; east to bluff Cut Hill - well okay not an especially stunning sight, but at nearly 2000 feet one of Dartmoor's highest and certainly loneliest places, the peaty hub from where the wandering spokes of streams flow to form so many of Devon's major rivers; and south to the craggy head of Great Mis Tor and the television mast on North Hessary Tor.

If after your earlier efforts your appetite remains whetted Cut Hill is an easy tramp less than a mile away, but allow 45 minutes or so for a round trip.

To return leave Fur Tor by walking north or north-east down its steep flank until the stream Cut Combe Water is reached. This should be followed to its meeting with the Amicombe and then downstream nearly to the Tavy, crossing where there is a large grassy island in the stream bed and so avoiding a long marshy section on the opposite bank.

Retrace your steps over Watern Oke the way you came, dropping down to the Tavy where it is joined by Rattle Brook.

Now the return route is the same as for the short-loopers. Cross Rattle Brook and walk upstream until it is met by a steeply descending stream from the left - Deadlake - at the appropriately named Deadlake Foot. This should then be followed until near its head when having passed through a small cutting Hare Tor is just left and south-west.

Having climbed Hare Tor either strike directly for the glorious views that Ger Tor has to offer over Mary Tavy, Plymouth Sound, and into Cornwall, or alternatively, if you can bear the idea of walking downhill only to have to return, head for the second tor of the five from the southern entrance to Tavy Cleave.

This tor affords a spectacular eagle's eye of the Tavy's gorge.

After a protracted linger, rather than making a bee-line for Ger Tor which involves the unnecessary loss of too much height, follow the contours round. Upon reaching Ger Tor, Lanehead is directly below with the leat being crossed by a small bridge.

---

39. NORTH DARTMOOR:
To Dartmoor's roof via the West Okement, High Willhays, Yes Tor and the Red-a-ven Brook - 9 miles

---

Directions

Start: Meldon Reservoir, near Okehampton.

Outline and
walk length: Upstream following the course of the West Okement, passing ancient high altitude oak-woodland and onto the wild moor surrounding Dartmoor's highest point. Lots of interesting industrial remains at the foot of Meldon Reservoir, so with

	explorations it is worth allowing five hours for the 9 mile walk.
Getting there:	Out of Okehampton follow signs to Meldon, passing through a small cluster of houses and going left uphill under the old railway bridge to Meldon Reservoir.
Parking:	Meldon Reservoir car park, with toilets.
Refreshments:	None on route.
Map:	OS 1:25,000 Dartmoor; Outdoor Leisure no. 28.
Warning:	This walk passes through the Okehampton army range. If a red flag is flying over the range firing is in progress. Firing dates and times, which include night firing, are given in many local papers. To be certain no firing is taking place telephone the range information line on Exeter 70164/ Okehampton 52939/Plymouth 501478/Torquay 294592, or the daily update on (01837) 52241/41 extension 3210, before you set out.

If there is one area of Dartmoor that comes closest to scenery on the grand scale it is the north-west corner. Here are found its highest peaks High Willhays at 2038 feet and Yes Tor at 2030 feet. At their foot lies the remarkable valley of the West Okement River. The valley is particularly straight as it follows a geological fault line but its U-shape and bare rock on the steep north facing wall present compelling evidence of glaciation even though the ice sheet of the last Ice Age never came this far south.

Mining and nascent industrialisation also feature on this route. At the foot of the Red-a-ven there is plenty evidence of quarrying past and present as well as mine adits. If you are lucky you may be able to find the broken products of a glass factory which operated here in the 19th century.

Leave the car park and turn left towards the reservoir, crossing it via the walkway over the dam wall. At the wall's end turn right. The path follows a fence, skirting the dark waters of the reservoir on your right. In spate a noisy waterfall tumbles from Homerton Hill on your left. Where the waters tail off at Vellake Corner keep left, cutting off a small grassy plain, and rejoin the West Okement on your right where the path joins a rising rough stony track.

The last dam to be built on Dartmoor, Meldon opened in 1972 and flooded what was reputedly one of the most dramatic and beautiful valleys on the whole moor. Crossing its walkway makes for a dizzying contrast. Downstream a drop of 181 feet, upstream a black lake vividly dotted in

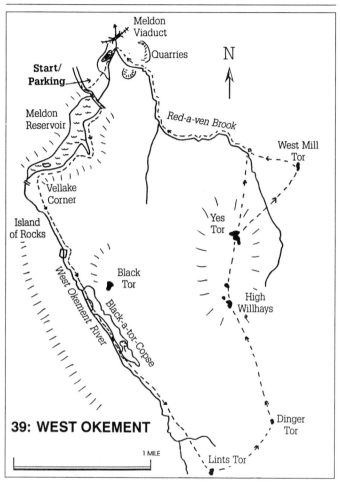

Meldon
Viaduct

Quarries

N

**Start/
Parking**

Meldon
Reservoir

Red-a-ven Brook

West Mill
Tor

Vellake
Corner

Yes
Tor

Island
of Rocks

West Okement River

Black
Tor

Black-a-tor Copse

High
Willhays

39: WEST OKEMENT

Dinger
Tor

1 MILE

Lints Tor

summer with wind-surfers. *During drought years when the waters drain
away, an island near the reservoir's tail can once again be reached on foot.*

Immediately after Vellake Corner the West Okement disappears under
a mass of boulders named by moormen 'The Island of Rocks', according to
William Crossing. In spate the river roars over a series of rapids and

squeezes round enormous boulders dumped upon its bed - testimony to its storm force. Drop down under the canopy of low oaks to sample this sudden raucous concentration of natural energy.

Leaving the Island of Rocks behind return to the track which climbs and once again becomes a path following the river. It makes a small diversion around a walled weir but otherwise its route is true if at times faint under the oaks of Black-a-tor-Copse, where care needs to be taken over moss covered boulders. Followed the path to the foot of Lints Tor at the valley's head.

Black-a-tor-Copse is one of the last three vestiges of high altitude oak-woodland that used to cloak much of Dartmoor, the other two being Wistman's Wood near Two Bridges and Piles Copse, on the River Erme. Under the gnarled twisted branches of its canopy there is a world far removed in spirit and physical appearance from the surrounding open moor. Guarding its north-east flank Black Tor rises like a shattered castle.

As you look upstream you may catch from the corner of your eye the glint of the Slipper Stones on the north-east facing flank of the valley. These are great slabs of exposed granite near the valley side's summit and steepest section. Stripped of vegetation, as a skeleton scoured of flesh, they blaze bone white in the sun, or glisten where water leaks over their surface from the bog above.

A glorious valley unmatched in scale anywhere else on Dartmoor. A few oaks survive detached from the main body of the copse, clinging to life amid the dense litter-cum-scree slopes.

At the foot of Lints Tor the West Okement begins to turn south. Leave it and strike out ahead uphill for the short pull over rough ground to Lints Tor.

The Tor is not especially impressive, a narrow tower badly undercut on one side. Yet the views downstream are truly rewarding and make for a good journey's break.

Upon leaving do not head directly north for High Willhays; this will only take you immediately into a boggy. Instead head due east along a faint path and upon reaching the hillside opposite swing due north-east towards Dinger Tor. This is not the most direct route to the summit of High Willhays, but by looping round the back you should avoid the worst of a boggy area west of Dinger Tor. Almost directly east of Lints Tor is a set of flooded turf-ties.

Dinger Tor barely qualifies for the title, so you will not be missing much if you turn uphill due north-west to High Willhays before you reach it. From High Willhays walk north to Yes Tor.

After half a mile of heather and grass, where red grouse whirr in ground hugging flight, you will come to the unimposing roof of Dartmoor, High Willhays - the highest point in southern England. While the summit itself hardly inspires awe the bleak empty landscape of north Dartmoor spreads away to the east and south. Looking west the view stretches to the Cornish hills and Bodmin Moor.

It is a short stride north over the col linking High Willhays to its more impressive looking, though lower neighbour, Yes Tor.

Dreadful army roads and tracks criss-cross this, the wildest area of Dartmoor's high moor. Yes Tor is painted a rather over-brilliant white to distinguish its triangulation point and into its side one of the more discreet army observation posts is built.

Leaving Yes Tor for the return, head due north-east if you want to bag West Mill Tor - or alternatively head due north, directly downhill to reach a small pool and wall. This is the Red-a-ven Brook, which you should follow downstream along its tight secluded valley, keeping it on your left.

As you descend so granite is left behind and replaced by metamorphosed Meldon Slates - the change marked by small scree slopes on the right bank.

The path passes a low mound - all that remains of an old copper mine - before entering a wide area heavily scarred by quarries and industrial activity. Flat-topped spoil heaps fan out from the aplite quarries on the left. Aplite was used in the manufacture of glass, and during the last century a bottle factory was sited in this area; its products were said at the time to rival those of Dresden. Looking north Meldon Viaduct is an impressive engineering feat: now occasionally used by bungee jumpers plunging on their elasticated falls. Beyond the rail viaduct is Meldon Quarry where hard dolerite is blasted for use in road building.

Cross the West Okement below the dam by a small footbridge. Once on the path if you turn right and duck under the trees you will come to a now flooded limestone quarry with kilns nearby.

To return follow the footpath uphill, passing an old adit shaft on your right. Once out of the woods strike out directly uphill through a field: shortly you will find a wall on your right which will bring you out east of the car park.

---

40. NORTH DARTMOOR:
The bleak lands - Scorhill, Teignhead Farm, Watern Tor,
via the River North Teign - 9.5 miles

Directions

Start: Scorhill, near Gidleigh west of Chagford.

Outline and
walk length: Out along the River Teign to the 'hidden' waterfall at Manga Hole and onto the ruin of Teignhead Farm. An extension to the twin stone circles at Grey Wethers returning over open moor via Watern Tor. Take a compass and know how to use it. If the weather is foul it is easy enough to return along the River Teign. Allow five hours for the 9.5 mile walk. If you begin at Gidleigh, by adding Walk 33 to the route you can make a 15 mile walk.

Getting there: Signs to Gidleigh from the A382 Moretonhampstead road.

Parking: Small car park at Scorhill. Rather than turning left into Gidleigh keep straight on, keeping left at the next junction and turning right above Berrydown, the road signposted as a no through road.

Map: OS 1:25,000 Outdoor Leisure no. 28 Dartmoor.

Warning: Watern Tor is just outside the Okehampton army range. If a red flag is flying over the range firing is in progress. Firing dates and times, which include night firing, are given in many local papers. To be certain no firing is taking place telephone the range information line on Exeter 70164/ Okehampton 52939/Plymouth 501478/Torquay 294592, or the daily update on (01837) 52241/41 extension 3210, before you set out.

Leaving Scorhill car park walking uphill, pass through the gate and you are onto the moor in all its bleakness. Follow the track straight ahead over Scorhill Down in front of you, past Scorhill Circle, and head straight for the River Teign. There is plenty to explore here and you will find all the information in the Gidleigh/Kestor Walk no. 33.

At this point the Teign sweeps across a wide plain before plunging off the moor to begin its sprint to the sea. This is awkward boggy ground but unavoidable. Keep the river on your left as you walk upstream. Leave it where it takes a 90 degree turn left. Instead head straight on - for a short way there is a track to follow - and aim for the edge of the high ground opposite, close to where the river enters the marshy plain. In this way you walk the long side of a triangle instead of the other two sides formed by the river, and at least minimise the worst of the wet going.

This section of the route out and back is tiresome but occasionally it has

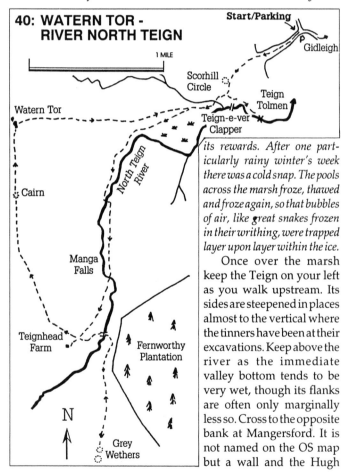

40: WATERN TOR - RIVER NORTH TEIGN

Start/Parking

Gidleigh

1 MILE

Scorhill Circle

Watern Tor

Teign Tolmen

Teign-e-ver Clapper

North Teign River

Cairn

Manga Falls

Teignhead Farm

Fernworthy Plantation

N

Grey Wethers

its rewards. After one particularly rainy winter's week there was a cold snap. The pools across the marsh froze, thawed and froze again, so that bubbles of air, like great snakes frozen in their writhing, were trapped layer upon layer within the ice.

Once over the marsh keep the Teign on your left as you walk upstream. Its sides are steepened in places almost to the vertical where the tinners have been at their excavations. Keep above the river as the immediate valley bottom tends to be very wet, though its flanks are often only marginally less so. Cross to the opposite bank at Mangersford. It is not named on the OS map but a wall and the Hugh

Lake stream meet the Teign which is crossed by a metal barred fence and stepping stones where you cross. If the stones are covered the river can be traversed with care by edging along the lower rung of a metal round-barred fence which crosses the Teign from bank to bank.

Even when not in spate the Teign valley has tricks to play upon the unwary. One morning while approaching the fence at Mangersford I completely missed a small but, as it turned out, very deep bog fed by Hugh Lake. Before I knew it I had the greatest of shocks as the ground disappeared beneath me and I found myself up to my thighs in black ooze. You have been warned.

Having crossed the river a stile will carry you over the wall before the valley sides rapidly steepen. A wall on your right will be between you and the river. Soon the Teign is rushing through a gully known as Manga Hole. At its head you may be surprised to hear the rush of a waterfall. Unmarked on any OS map, this is Manga Falls.

A fantastically wild place in spate. The Teign crashes over boulders, choking the falls' entrance, and echoes off steep valley sides. In places the river slides over broad sheets of exposed granite. Where the water has forced its way between the plates, with the swirling, grinding action of suspended gravels, holes 2 feet deep but only inches wide have been cut. Gazing downstream Manga Hole looks even more dramatic.

At the head of the waterfall where the river is narrowest it is easy to cross to the opposite side and then, via a ladder-stile, the wall which lines the bank. A path rises diagonally left from the river and leads to the ruin of Teignhead Farm.

A desperately lonely place built between 1780 and 1840, Teignhead Farm was cut off for weeks at a time in winter. The ruins are being gradually reclaimed by the moor, their occupants having long given up the struggle.

Now the farm faces the grim coniferous ranks of Fernworthy Forest, its own small adjacent plantation having been felled in the last few years. Nevertheless Teignhead retains an "oasis" feel - the few bright green grassy fields close by contrast with the bleakness of the surrounding moorland.

Though a ruin the farm was habitable and roofed up to the 1960s when it was deliberately dismantled to discourage people from trying to claim "squatters' rights" and gain occupancy. The shell complete with its fireplace and what could be a tinners' mould is worth exploring. Look also

171

at the L-notched gate post, an old Dartmoor-type gateway into which planks or bars of wood were slotted.

An extension for the fit and well worth a visit about a mile away are Grey Wethers stone circles, the largest two complete (though restored by Victorian archaeologists) stone circles on Dartmoor. The south circle is 116 feet 6 inches in diameter and the north circle 103 feet 6 inches. Unusually for Dartmoor stone circles the stones are generally flat-topped, mostly broad and substantial. A wether, you may be interested to learn, is a castrated ram.

Grey Wethers can be reached by crossing the River Teign by the clapper bridge and following the gently rising broad track due south, roughly parallel with the plantation. Retrace your footsteps to Teignhead Farm for the main walk's return leg.

If the weather is bad and your map and compass skills limited, return via the river. If not, just north of Teignhead Farm is a small stream, Manga Brook, which you should follow upstream. You will pass various mounds thrown up by the tinners until the brook crosses a low and tumbledown wall. Though faint and in places no more than a low grassy bank you should turn right to follow this bank uphill. Eventually it meets a much larger wall and stile which you should cross.

Ahead and due north is a cairn, an ancient burial mound, despoiled long ago by the treasure hunters of previous centuries. Pick your way to the top of this pile of loose stones. Beyond is Watern Tor about a quarter of a mile away and a quick tramp, while glorious views open out all round.

Watern Tor is split into a number of outcrops. Two of them lean, their heads bowed together almost touching, to leave a giant opening between - the Thirlestone (literally a gateway or portal) - through which it is possible to pass. On a clear day the views are wonderful with the full sweep of the River Teign immediately below and in the distance Chagford to the east.

On returning to Scorhill one summer's evening I turned to watch the sunset - Watern Tor was silhouetted and through the Thirlestone a single jewel of light pierced the gathering gloom.

The return from Watern is a direct if dull yomp. Strike out due east for the River Teign about a mile away, skirting the marsh the way you came. Retrace your steps back to Scorhill Circle, over Scorhill Down, and leave the moor via the track between the walled fields back to the car park.

---

41. NORTH DARTMOOR:
The quiet byways between Hennock and Lustleigh - 10 miles.

Directions

Start:	Hennock, west of the River Teign near Bovey Tracey.
Outline and walk length:	Plenty of interest for the mine archaeologist in this little visited area of Mid Devon on Dartmoor's edge. Some 10 miles of woodland footpath and country lane walking including a few gentle and not so gentle climbs. Allow five to six hours, especially if you spend time exploring Hennock and Lustleigh.
Getting there:	Hennock is 14 miles from Exeter. Follow the A38 turning off onto the B3193 signposted Teign Valley. After the quarry take the first left which is signposted to Hennock and Teign Village.
Parking:	At the top end of the village past the church, opposite what was once a chapel.
Refreshments:	In Hennock the Palk Arms, which has great views to Haldon, and a general store. Otherwise none on walk unless you make a short extension to Lustleigh where the Cleave pub and various stores can be found.
Map:	If you use 1:25,000, the walk is over two maps, the OS Dunsford and Kenton, and the OS Dartmoor map in their Outdoor Leisure series. The OS 1:50,000 Okehampton map covers the route but lacks detail.

Called Hainoc in the Domesday Book, Hennock retains an atmosphere that is at once timeless, remote and peaceful - despite being only 3 miles from the busy A38.

It was not always so quiet. Last century the Teign Valley stretching from Hennock to Dunsford was pock-marked with small copper, lead, iron, manganese and silver mines.

With chimneys and rough buildings suddenly erupting from hillsides the mines were fitfully worked until the profits promised to speculators failed to materialise and the mines sank back into the thicket undergrowth. In Hennock a few of the original miners' cottages remain on the left as you leave the village beyond the church near the converted chapel.

The last of the valley's mines, Greatrock, near Hennock, clung on until 1970, bringing down the curtain upon centuries of shaft mining in Devon. During Greatrock's life miners raised to the surface a glittering grey ore, micaceous haematite, also known as "shining or looking-glass ore" - a type of iron much in demand as a constituent of weather-proofing paint for tools ranging from spades to battleships. Ore samples can easily be found en route.

Before setting off it is worth wandering around Hennock.

The compact granite Church of St. Mary should not be missed. It mostly dates from 1450, though the tower was probably built in 1250 - quite how the congregation felt about a two hundred year wait for the rest of the church is not recorded.

Inside there is a stunning ceiling or ceilure of brilliant blue and gilt, but of most interest is the crudely painted 15th century rood screen depicting a number of rather curious characters and scenes on its panels. One shows a lady - two rats clinging by their mouths to her cape; on another a gentleman holds a large rat over a boot - a reference to the Black Death?

On leaving the church turn left and walk gently uphill (back to where you will have parked). The road runs out at a sign that announces that the track in front is for access and pedestrians only. Follow this track and at its top follow the path as marked left across

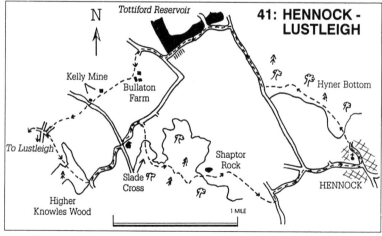

a field - noting the views over to Haldon and the white tower of Lawrence Castle - and then down a short but steep wooded hill.

You will come out below Great Rock Farm. Turn right and then almost immediately left up a signposted footpath. As you climb a view down the steep combe of Hyner Bottom opens out. About halfway up, the path runs over a spoil heap of micaceous haematite ore. If you're tempted to remove samples it is wise to wrap them because they flake into a powder at the slightest touch.

Along the path there are a number of iron-grated air valves hissing eerily - though rather prosaically they are linked to the nearby Kennick and Tottiford reservoirs. Over a rise the path starts to fall past a small stand of gloomy fir trees and rocky outcrops. At the path's foot bear left onto a track and then right over Beadon Brook via a wooden footbridge - having crossed which, turn left and you will leave Netton Cleave coming out onto a lane.

Turn right uphill and beware what little traffic comes this way. There is a short sharp climb before a junction where you go left. Pass downhill under coniferous trees and at the next junction go left again. Tottiford Reservoir will be on your right as you pass over the dam wall. Keep straight on - which means in effect bearing right at the next junction - and gently uphill before turning left down a public bridleway signposted as coming out near Kelly.

At Bullaton Farm turn right uphill before the farm buildings through three gates, so that the farm is on your left.

At Bullaton Farm before you turn right walk a little further along the farm lane until you reach a small, rather curious-looking grassy pitched-roofed granite building, on the left. This is an ash house where ash from the farm's domestic fires was stored. Later the ash would have been strewn on the farm vegetable garden in place of the artificial fertilisers which were to supersede it from the mid 19th century onwards.

Returning to the path notice a heavy iron wheel high up on the barn wall - part of an old threshing machine. Also on your left are two rather unusual circular granite plinths raised 2 to 3 feet above the ground - possibly unique in this form in Devon, these are rick stands used for storing drying hay.

After the third gate follow the sign pointing to the right-hand opposite corner of the field, through another gate, and downhill under lush woodland the path marked by red and blue painted spots.

Flickering jewels dance across the path as rare spears of sunlight pierce the dense tree canopy's silent gloom. From a broken cottage, its garden choked with nettles, hemmed in by thickening trunks, a startled crow fled, its wings catching the sun in blaze of midnight iridescence.

This cottage, its roof fallen in, was probably the home of the Kelly Mine manager. The mine was worked between 1879 and 1944. Its buildings, including the stamping house where the iron ore was crushed, are passed on the right where the path meets the A382.

At the bottom cross the A382 to the footpath opposite signposted to Lustleigh via Wrayland Barn. Through another gate keep the hedge on your right, crossing into the next field by a stile, still keeping the hedge on your right.

Part way along, go right over a stile and cross two fields diagonally by a path barely discernible in the grass. In the left corner of the second field look for the oak tree clearly marked with a yellow spot; go up the path as marked. Cross onto another path by a stile at the end of which turn left in front of a large white house. If you wish to visit Lustleigh (Walk no. 34) turn right, left and right again along the road.

Otherwise having gone left at the white house walk uphill signposted to Hatherleigh. Ignore the two right tracks and gated track left, instead following the well-vegetated path thick with the scent of blossom and insects busy with pollen. As the path climbs it becomes increasingly enclosed and shaded; underfoot there are fewer plants clawing at your boots.

At the path summit cross into Higher Knowles Wood by a stile. Through the wood turn left onto a lane which will bring you back to the A382. Cross directly over up a lane at Slade Cross, walk a short way uphill turning right just beyond a barn where signposted "County Road near Higher Bowden".

The path is a wide dusty track. After a few strides cross the stile left round the gate blocking the track which you once again follow. Leaving the farm behind on the right the track comes to a junction. Take the left path which runs between a hillside of bracken on the left and hedge right. At the next stile cross and drop down to the electric fence which runs parallel to a track, which still running ahead you cross onto by a stile on the right. Follow the track to its end following the fence on the left. At the track's end turn right as signposted. After 5 yards turn left through a gate marked with a

Hennock

prominent "Footpath" sign in yellow. Follow the hedge on your right. You are now just north of the remains of an old tuberculosis hospital now being developed for housing.

You will come to a gate between a wall falling from the left and the hedge. Go over the gate via a stile. The path is in deep gloom with tall stands of nettle for company and it falls to another stile which you cross and bear left towards an isolated stand of fir trees. A signpost directs you to the left of these. On your right you will see a rectangle of asphalt which used to be a tennis court. Walk gently uphill. A thick coniferous plantation will be on your left. Shortly the path enters the plantation, turns to the right and crosses a brook. It climbs, clearly signposted, uphill under fir trees, passing a sign stating "Hawkmoor Water Supply" and over a stile into Shaptor Woods.

Beware the fenced off mine shafts. Where two footpaths cross go left, still signposted to Higher Bowden. Shortly the path bears right and on your left the barren granite dome of Shaptor Rocks rears into sight.

A path runs to the summit of this bluff hill from where there are fine views over Bovey Tracey and, south-west, Haytor Rocks. Retracing your steps, follow the main path, exiting the woods by a stile. You will then be confronted by three more stiles in quick succession before bearing left and crossing a fifth stile.

Once over, head straight on along the path opposite. After a while the path passes into and (via a stile) out of a wood. Cross the field that you have now entered, and over the walk's final stile enter the lane.

Turn left and then immediately right nearly opposite Higher Bowden. At the next junction another right will bring you, less than half a mile later, back to Hennock.

---

42. SOUTH DARTMOOR:
A tramp to the summit of the southern moor at Ryder's Hill - 5 miles.

Directions

Start: Michelcombe, near Holne, west of Ashburton.

Outline and
walk length: A little over 5 miles, half uphill over open moorland to Ryder's Hill, the highest point on the southern moor. Allow two to three hours.

Getting there: From the A38 exit at the southern end of Ashburton following signs to Holne. Pass through the village onto Michelcombe.

Parking: Wide verge in Michelcombe on the left just over the bridge, though space is very limited. Be careful not to block the farm and do not park on the bridlepath. If you have to park back in Holne, it adds an extra mile of lane walking.

Refreshments: None on walk. Nearest at Holne: Old Forge Cream Teas, Church House Inn and post office. Also pub nearby in Scorriton.

Map: OS 1:25,000 Dartmoor; Outdoor Leisure no. 28.

Michelcombe, or Mutchecum, as William Crossing writing at the turn of the century claimed it was called by its inhabitants, is highly picturesque. A number of cottages cluster round a farm, some in a rather down at heel state, yet to be gentrified.

178

Nearby flows the Holy Brook in its tight valley, and between the farm and cottages an old moorland track, the Sandy Way. Ryder's Hill, at 1690 feet, is the highest point on southern Dartmoor, and the walk's goal. If the ascent seems daunting, spare a thought for the tin miners who used to "commute" weekly in all weathers on foot from moorland fringe towns like Buckfastleigh to the mines of Holne Moor and the River Swincombe valley via the Sandy Way.

Climb out of Michelcombe along the Sandy Way, here marked on the map as a bridlepath. After about half a mile you will pass through a gate onto the open moor. Ahead, the track, now grassy, leads directly uphill and bears slightly to the right. By a wind blasted rowan the path crosses the now-dry course of the Wheal Emma leat.

Cut in 1859, this leat drew water from the River Swincombe and contoured around Holne Moor some 10 miles to deliver its contents into the River Mardle - the increase in flow was needed to drive a waterwheel at the Brookwood mine keeping the shafts pumped dry.

Looking back Michelcombe nestles in its valley. In the distance the Teign estuary glistens like a pond, with the sea beyond. Craggy tors stud the northern moor, scudding cloud sending lakes of light and dark across the heather. The Dart Gorge rents the granite massif, dividing absolutely the north and south upland.

After a short distance the path's ascent becomes much more gentle. Bearing right, you will reach a series of cuttings, spoil heaps and roofless buildings. Ringleshutts - the name conjuring up the image of an unpleasant medieval skin disease - is a disused tin mine. The ruined buildings make a sheltered spot for a break. Looking

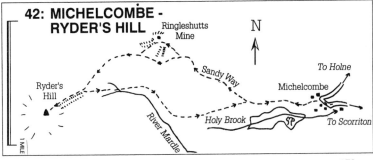

179

north-east, a mile or so away is Venford Reservoir.

To continue the walk, head due south-west across the workings, rejoining Sandy Way and heading once again uphill. You should see about half a mile away and to the south-west another cutting, running uphill: this you aim for, walking first west then south, so as to avoid dropping into Mardle Head. On reaching the cutting follow it to its end, the top of which will bring you nearly to the summit of Ryder's Hill, a few strides away.

In itself Ryder's Hill is a disappointment but on a clear day the panoramic views are wonderful. Portland is a possibility with the whole sweep of the Devon and Dorset coasts in between. Nearer at hand, across an unbroken expanse of featureless moor, is the main spoil heap of the disused Redlake China Clay Works. To the north are all manner of tors - Great Mis Tor, Bellever, Hameldon and more.

Now for the easy bit - the return, which is all downhill. Return to the cutting, following it downhill to Mardle Head. Keep to the left of this nascent river - not in the valley bottom, instead just above the various overgrown heaps of rubble that attest to tinners' streaming operations.

There is a rough path to follow here, and as the Mardle descends to your right, follow the contours round left along the path, dropping down to the course of the Wheal Emma leat, which can be crossed by a now redundant footbridge.

A clear path now descends gently through stands of hawthorn to the gate that, many expended calories earlier, you passed through on the way to Ringleshutts. And so, by the bridlepath, return to Michelcombe.

---

43. SOUTH DARTMOOR:
**Where Dartmoor is most forbidding - from Princetown along the old Great Western Railway track.
A linear or round route - both 6 miles**

Direction

Start: Princetown, Dartmoor.

Outline and walk length: An easy to follow, easy to walk route along the bed of the disused Great Western Princetown rail line. Disused quarries and tors passed on the way. The route can either be walked as a linear 6 miles ending at the car park and bus stop at Sharpitor or as a round 6 miles returning by the path south of Swelltor Quarries and missing out Ingra Tor. Allow two to three hours as there is plenty to explore.

Getting there: Princetown is on the transmoor B3212 road.

Parking: Free car park in Princetown near the National Park Information Centre.

By bus: Transmoor Link, service No. 82, contact Devon General. Refreshments: Plenty of pubs and various stores in Princetown. None on walk.

Map: OS 1:25,000 Dartmoor; Outdoor Leisure no. 28.

W.G. Hoskins described Princetown as "a grim little town some 1,400 feet above sea level, with an abominable climate of fog, snow, wind, and more than 80 inches of cold rain". Grateful residents now celebrate this homely place and its founder, Sir Thomas Tyrwhitt, with a series of signposted walks of the same name round the town. Ever the enthusiast Sir Thomas began farming the surrounding moor as early as 1780, believing lush pastures were for the taking but for a little agricultural application. He also had Dartmoor Prison built in 1806, for which thousands of inmates have shown scant gratitude ever since.

Dartmoor is pitted with small quarries that supplied local needs but with the onset of the 19th century, larger commercial developments appeared. Sir Thomas owned the quarries on Walkhampton Common, near to the town, and their growth was spurred by the opening of the Plymouth and Dartmoor tramway up to Princetown in 1823. This later became the Princetown branch line of the Great Western Railway, when a new track was opened in 1882. Quarries at Foggintor, Swelltor, Heckwood and Ingra Tor all thrived, even into the first half of the 20th century.

Now this area of the moor is once again silent, the sound of steam jacks and splitting granite consigned to the past. The railway line was removed with its closure to public engines in 1956 and it now offers the walker its gentle old course from Princetown to the quarries and beyond. It may be walked as a linear route ending at Sharpitor where a bus back to Princetown or Exeter can be caught, or as a round.

Out of the car park turn left, south-west, away from the town and onto a road that is part of one of the eponymous Tyrwhitt's trails. Carry straight on past Princetown fire station on your left. This is the course of the old Princetown railway and the route, soon a path,

181

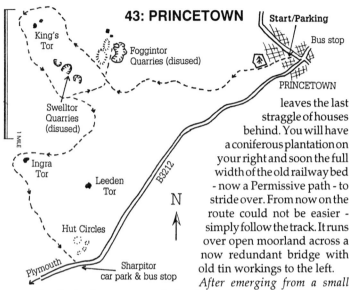

43: PRINCETOWN

Start/Parking

Bus stop

King's Tor

Foggintor Quarries (disused)

PRINCETOWN

Swelltor Quarries (disused)

1 MILE

Ingra Tor

Leeden Tor

B3212

N

Hut Circles

Plymouth

Sharpitor car park & bus stop

leaves the last straggle of houses behind. You will have a coniferous plantation on your right and soon the full width of the old railway bed - now a Permissive path - to stride over. From now on the route could not be easier - simply follow the track. It runs over open moorland across a now redundant bridge with old tin workings to the left.

After emerging from a small cutting the track sweeps around a bend so that, some 200 feet below, you can see its course as it skirts Ingra Tor. In the distance is Plymouth Sound, the city and farther west the Cornish Hills. In the foreground lies the valley of the River Walkham and south Burrator reservoir, girded by the rocky pinnacles of Sharpitor and Sheeps Tor.

Worth exploring round a bend in the line is Foggintor Quarry. Here there are traces of the old railway sidings. On the right is the entry into the quarry pit itself, its mouth marked by a few bricks of what was the smithy. Part of the quarry is now flooded, its waters sheltered by the surrounding granite walls. Nearby there are huge piles of granite spoil and the remains of what was the small quarry settlement. The last now demolished cottage was still lived in up to 1951.

Below one of the building shells, possibly the quarry manager's house, near some withered and blasted hawthorn trees, is a rubbish tip, where you can find broken bottles, jars and plates.

Foggintor closed at Christmas 1906 with the quarrymen transferring to the other nearby granite workings. The last of these, Ingra Tor Quarry, closed in the 1930s.

To the north is a parade of tors: Cox Tor, Great Staple Tor, and Great

*Granite spoil and quarry buildings at Foggintor Quarry with
Great Mis Tor in the distance*

*Mis Tor. Below them is the new gouge that is Merrivale Quarry - the last
working quarry on Dartmoor.*

On leaving the quarry rejoin and follow the rail track. You may
feel under foot the imprint of removed sleepers. As you approach
King's Tor, scattered around on the right are squares of fire bricks,
presumably from the boilers of the steam derricks and cranes that
used to work the quarries. The track takes a huge loop around
King's Tor as it slowly descends, turning back on itself at Swelltor
Quarry. Here the remains of an inclined plane can be seen, the
trucks moved up and down with the aid of iron rollers and chains.

On the left is a track that returns to Foggintor. Follow this to
make a round route back to Princetown. Otherwise follow the old
line over another bridge and around Ingra Tor. Beyond the tor there
is a track which branches off left roughly at right angles and runs
uphill to rejoin the road at a car park below Sharpitor. The bus stop
is nearby.

---

44. SOUTH DARTMOOR:
Medieval warrens and the Moor's tallest standing stone - along the River Plym. Ridge and river route - 9 miles

---

Directions

Start: Cadover Bridge, Shaugh Prior, near Plymouth on the south-western edge of Dartmoor.

Outline and
walk length: Low level moorland walking, mostly along clearly defined paths through the River Plym valley. Allow four hours for the 9 miles - longer for explorations of the prehistoric and more recent historical remains.

Getting there: On the road between Meavy and Shaugh Prior.

Parking: Car park at Cadover Bridge.

Refreshments: None on walk.

Map: OS 1:25,000 Dartmoor; Outdoor Leisure no. 28.

There is no greater concentration of prehistoric remains, hut circles, ancient field systems and stone rows on Dartmoor than in the valley of the River Plym where they date to about 2500 BC. The Drizzlecombe Menhir at 14 feet high is the tallest on the moor.

Later inhabitants have further exploited the valley. The old tinners set to work diverting the Plym's flow cutting into the bank and leaving their tell-tale spoil mounds. Shaft tin miners worked later. Eylesbarrow Tin Mine, the walk's northernmost point, closed in 1852 and 8 feet of the shaft is still visible along with various other mine features.

The valley is dotted with warrens which flourished from medieval times to the 1950s. Warreners operated from Brisworthy, Trowlesworthy, Legistor Warren, lonely Ditsworthy and Hentor. "Pillow mounds," artificial buries consisting of long down-slope banks of stone and soil drained by a perimeter ditch, were thrown up by the warreners for their rabbits. During hard winters they even put out food for their small herbivores. Warreners went to great lengths to protect their rabbits - even building ingenious granite traps to capture "vermin" like stoats and weasels.

The rabbits were caught with nets, their skins going off for the fur trade and their meat to market. The trade collapsed as an exploding rabbit population in the general countryside made dedicated warrening uneconomic combined with the fall of rabbit as a staple meat dish.

More recently the land immediately south where the Plym leaves the National Park has been extensively quarried for china clay. The middle reach of the Plym itself hides more huge deposits but a combination of National Trust and National Park control should ensure the valley's security.

From the car park south of Cadover Bridge cross the bridge turning immediately right passing through a smaller car park and following

44: RIVER PLYM

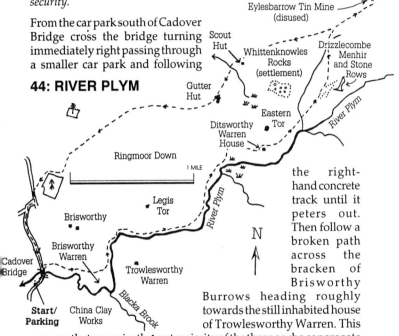

the right-hand concrete track until it peters out. Then follow a broken path across the bracken of Brisworthy Burrows heading roughly towards the still inhabited house of Trowlesworthy Warren. This ensures that you miss the vast majority of the throng who congregate by Blacka Brook Foot.

With the Plym on your right walk upstream. The path is easy to follow. After less than half a mile it leaves the narrow confines of granite walls and enters the open moor, passing the first grassy mounds left by tinners. Legis Tor is to your left.

Listen out for the moorland birds, especially wheatear, meadow pipit, stonechat and the trilling skylark. Continue upstream along the path which leaves the Plym south of Ditsworthy Warren to skirt a broad marshy plain.

A timeless scene on the Plym with Ditsworthy Warren in the background

Ditsworthy Warren House is nowadays shuttered and sealed with iron bars. Occasionally it is used by the military for training exercises - the oil drum with "BRNC Bomb Exercise" painted on the side being something of a pointer to Britannia Royal Naval College in Dartmouth. Blasted pine, fir and ash trees scarcely break the west wind but the most fascinating feature of the warren are the three granite dog kennels built into the wall of the pen immediately north of the house.

From Ditsworthy follow the path due north of the house, once again upstream but this time a couple of hundred yards west and above the Plym. Break off from the path and make for the first large standing stone at the southern end of the stone row whose most famous member is the Drizzlecombe Menhir. Close to hand on the opposite side of Drizzle Combe, a small valley on the left, you should be able to make out the large prehistoric settlement of Whittenknowles. From the great menhir look downstream. Above the left bank and below Hentor Warren a distinct field system divided by low grassy banks can be seen where generations of oxen once hauled wooden ploughs.

From the menhir head due north into Drizzle Combe itself, crossing onto the path which climbs and bears right, or to the north-east, to Eylesbarrow Tin Mine.

From the mine retrace your steps down the broad grassy path. Instead of heading back down Drizzle Combe keep straight on roughly towards Gutter Tor. The path trends to the right of the tor. Keep to the right of a small fir plantation and scout hut marked on the map. After which cross the small stream emerging from Gutter Mire - another area heavily dug out and altered by the activity of tin miners - and climb to the summit of Gutter Tor. Approached from the north the tor looks passably impressive - but it is one of those granite piles which on the opposite side is practically grassed to its peak.

Note the stone basins with drainage lips cut deeply into the capping blocks of granite. And the view north-west is rather fine across to Sheeps Tor, Burrator Reservoir, Leather Tor and Sharpitor, with the Cornish Hills beyond.

Leaving Gutter Tor head due west along an indistinct path across barren moorland. The ground between Gutter Tor and the lane you will shortly come to is private land where access is of a permissive nature. The owner points out that dogs must be kept on leads at all times and that the estate has the right to close the route at any time. Ahead is Plymouth, its Sound and the sea. To your left you should be able to make out the low grassy ridge of an ancient boundary wall and beyond that a short stone row on Ringmoor Down. Follow the boundary as it drops south-west and then strike out for Brisworthy Plantation. Upon reaching the eastern corner go right so that the plantation is on your left. At its end turn left and via a track onto a lane. Go left, walk downhill ignoring the turn-off for Brisworthy hamlet and at the next junction turn left back to Cadover Bridge.

---

45. SOUTH DARTMOOR:
The most perfect valley on the Moor - Harford to Red Lake returning along the River Erme. A ridge and river round - 12 miles

---

Directions

Start: Moorland car park above Harford, near Ivybridge, on the southern edge of Dartmoor.

Outline and
walk length: A brisk 12 miles of ridge and river walking, allow six hours. Out on the ridge, back by the river. Nearly half is along the

187

dry route of a disused narrow gauge railway with a return along part of the length of Dartmoor's longest stone row and the River Erme valley.

Getting there: Turn off the A38 Exeter-Plymouth road at the South Brent or Ivybridge junctions. From Ivybridge follow signs from the town to Harford. In Harford turn right before the church and drive uphill to the moorland car park.

Parking: As above.

Map: OS 1:25,000 Dartmoor; Outdoor Leisure no 28. Take a compass.

Bleak and featureless, I always find southern Dartmoor intimidating, especially if approached from the north near the Dart Gorge. From the south it is a different matter with the Rivers Avon, Erme, Yealm and Plym all supplying the walker with excellent routes into the interior. Turning off the busy A38 to follow the wandering lanes to Harford there is a palpable transition from the rush of the 20th century to a far older, less frantic rhythm.

The Erme valley is as rich in interest as anywhere on Dartmoor. Thick with the ruins of prehistoric settlement, the Moor's longest stone row running for two and a quarter miles and a host of tinners' workings. The eastern ridge above the Erme offers the easiest of paths along the bed of the disused narrow gauge Red Lake railway, past the wonderfully named Hobajons Cross and delightful Quickbeam Hill. The track ends at the now derelict Red Lake China Clay Works, the walk's halfway point.

From the moorland car park you should strike out north-east over short yellow grasses, uphill for Piles Hill. As you climb, the granite outcrop of Sharp Tor appears to your left, guarding the entrance of the Erme Valley under the lowering gaze of Stalldown Barrow opposite.

Hobajons Cross is passed on the way and at Piles Hill there is a small cairn, a low grassy barrow and a no-longer-standing standing stone. What looks like an intermittent stone row along the ridge is, in fact, a series of boundary stones dividing the parishes of Ugborough in the east from Harford in the west.

Just north you will come to the disused railway. Now it is a kind of walkers' motorway. Except for a short diversion half a mile on when you leave it (bearing off right for Three Barrows only to regain it near Left Lake Mires and a flooded clay pit) you can fold away

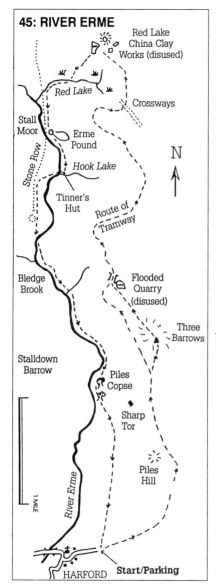

45: RIVER ERME

Red Lake
China Clay
Works (disused)

Red Lake

Crossways

Stall
Moor

Erme
Pound

Hook Lake

N

Stone Row

Tinner's
Hut

Route of
Tramway

Bledge
Brook

Flooded
Quarry
(disused)

Three
Barrows

Stalldown
Barrow

Piles
Copse

Sharp
Tor

Piles
Hill

River Erme

1 MILE

HARFORD

Start/Parking

your map until you reach the old china clay works at Red Lake.

Three Barrows is, as the name implies, three barrows or burial chambers, composed of heaped granite blocks and rubble. The summit has the added excitement of a triangulation point - from where there are fine views across the South Hams, Plymouth Sound, the undulating folds of moorland, as well as the despoliation caused by the quarries of Lee Moor.

Rejoining the track near Left Lake Mires a solid stone bridge carries the disused railway over a stream running from flooded clay workings. Look for two long, narrow, concrete settling tanks, square at one end, rounded at the other, associated with the workings. A mile further on where the track curves through 180 degrees forming a loop are the mica or "mikey" pits where the clay from the china clay works was pumped, washed and then piped to Bittaford. The northern head of the loop is called Crossways. From here bearing off south, horse drawn carriages used to carry peat down the old Zeal Tor tramway to the Shipley naphtha works on the banks of the River Avon.

The track sweeps round the contours revealing the conical spoil heap of Red Lake China Clay Works, a sight which I always find fascinating. It seems an eruption. Purple heather has colonised its slopes. Rainwater and footfalls have in turn cut deep cracks through to the white gritty spoil below. At a distance this gives the impression of a white lava spewed down a volcano's flanks. The notion that you have stumbled over a mini-volcano is further heightened by the lack of scale provided by any other feature. The clay works closed in 1932 but the ruins of the old steam engine house are still clearly visible at the railway's end. Now nature is reclaiming the broken quarry buildings, the modest pit workings flooded.

Do not make a bee-line for the spoil heap as a direct assault is wet underfoot and though the railway's bed floods in winter, it is infinitely preferable to pick your way along its side or upon the top of the cutting through which it now passes. The track may be longer in distance but is definitely shorter in time.

On leaving the spoil heap - a fine place for lunch if it is not too windy - make for the larger of the three flooded workings. Along the pit's southern edge, a cross-section of the peat in various stages of formation can be seen. It sits upon the gravel and clay that late last century turned this area into one of small-scale industrial activity.

The walk's return leg follows the Erme for most of the way. Head due south-west passing the flooded working on your right and another smaller spoil heap. Walk downhill, crossing Red Lake and its attendant bog to its left bank, upstream before it becomes too wet.

Red Lake, not a lake at all but a small stream, derives its name, depending on which authority you reach for, either from the abundance of red stemmed cotton-grass nodding over the bog or the red iron oxide deposits in the water that make it such a foul-looking concoction.

Once on its left bank follow it downstream until near its meeting point with the River Erme, where on your left, follow the rather overgrown stone row. This, the longest stone row on Dartmoor, runs almost without interruption for two and a quarter miles from the Dancers cairn or retaining circle above Erme Plains to a small cairn on Green Hill, crossing the River Erme on the way. Follow the stone row to where it crosses the Erme. Stay on the left bank following the river downstream to Erme Pound and beyond to the point where another stream, Hook Lake, joins the Erme.

One and a quarter acres in size, Erme Pound, like the other pounds on the moor, was established during the medieval period for the management

The 'volcanic' spoil heap at Red Lake China Clay Works

of the ancient Forest of Dartmoor - here cattle and ponies, unofficially pastured in the forest, were impounded during annual drifts. Unlike the others, though, Erme Pound was a substantial prehistoric settlement before its change of use 2000 years later. Hidden in the pound's wall there is a letter box with stamp.

Almost at the apex of a triangle of land where Hook Lake joins the Erme there is a particularly fine two roomed tinner's blowing house, where tin ore was smelted and the tin poured into small ingot moulds. Here the extensive mounds of tinners' rubble point to where they diverted the stream and river bed in their hunt for the valuable ore.

Cross the Erme, climb the opposite bank and follow the stone row south to its end at the Dancers.

At the Dancers' centre is a small barrow, surrounded by a 45 feet diameter stone circle. Tradition has it that the Dancers is named after a troop of Sabbath Day revellers who reckoned without a special someone's limited sense of humour and were duly turned to stone. The view down the Erme from the stones is rather fine.

Head downstream from the Dancers and return to the left bank of the Erme by crossing just north of Bledge Brook. The left bank, with the river on the right, is now your route back.

A narrow path leads through bracken to the edge of Piles Copse. Brown trout flicker through a still pool where a water abstraction weir has been thrown across the river.

Piles Copse is sister to the old oak woods at Wistman's Wood and Black-a-tor, but here the oaks are far taller. At dusk or early morning look out for foxes - they are most certainly about. Ubiquitous to the fast flowing clean rivers of the moor, the dry-backed dipper dips its white breast in the rapids.

The path crosses some wide expanses of lush grass. But do not slavishly follow the Erme. At a point where a bank lifts you up away from the river's edge look to climb uphill along a distinct path, with Sharp Tor on your left, out of the woodland and diagonally across the valley side.

The path passes a large hawthorn tree and meets a field wall at the point where it runs due south. Keep the wall on your right, leaving it only where it turns right through 90 degrees back towards the river - here carry straight on due south back to the moor car park.

On the way you will pass a particularly fine kistvaen. Typically 4 feet long by 2 feet wide these granite slab-lined small prehistoric burial chambers can be found across Dartmoor. Long since plundered for supposed treasure, originally it would have contained a small pottery urn holding the ashes of the dead.

* * *

BIBLIOGRAPHY

The Rev. Arthur J.C. Beddow - *A History of Bere Ferrers*. Second ed. 1986.

Brian Byng - *Dartmoor's Mysterious Megaliths*. Barron Jay Ltd.

William Crossing - *Gems in Granite Setting*. Devon Books 1986 (orig. pub. 1905).

William Crossing - *Guide to Dartmoor*. David and Charles. The 1912 edition reprinted 1976.

Eric Hemery - *High Dartmoor*. Robert Hale 1983.

W.G. Hoskins - *Devon*. Devon Books. Commemorative edition 1992.

R.B. Ivimey-Cook - *Atlas of the Devon Flora*. The Devonshire Association 1984.

Denis McCallum - *Walks in Tamar and Tavy Country*. Obelisk Publications 1992.

John W. Perkins - *Geology Explained in South and East Devon*. David and Charles 1971.

P.H.G. Richardson - *Mines of Dartmoor and the Tamar Valley After 1913*. The Northen Mine Research Society 1992.

George Thurlow - *Thurlow's Dartmoor Companion*. Peninsular Press 1993.

And countless church guides and National Trust leaflets.